THE BEST OF BRITISH COOKING

The Best of British Cooking

MARIKA HANBURY TENISON

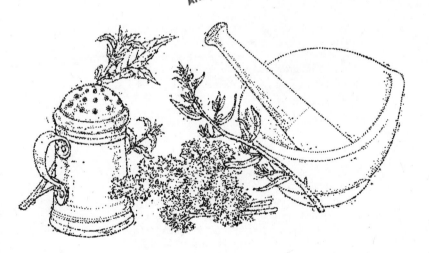

HART-DAVIS, MACGIBBON
GRANADA PUBLISHING
London Toronto Sydney New York

Published by Granada Publishing in
Hart-Davis, MacGibbon Ltd 1976
Second impression 1977

Granada Publishing Limited
Frogmore, St Albans, Herts AL2 2NF
and
3 Upper James Street, London W1R 4BP
1221 Avenue of the Americas, New York, NY 10020, USA
117 York Street, Sydney, NSW 2000, Australia
100 Skyway Avenue, Toronto, Ontario, Canada M9W 3A6
Trio City, Coventry Street, Johannesburg 2001, South Africa

ISBN 0 246 10935 1

Printed in Great Britain by
Fletcher & Son Ltd, Norwich

Set in Monotype Perpetua

CONTENTS

Foreword

Chapter 1 : Stocks and Soups

Chapter 2 : Fish

Chapter 3 : Meat

Chapter 4 : Poultry and Game

Chapter 5 : Vegetables

Chapter 6: Luncheon and Supper Dishes

Chapter 7: Sauces and Things

Chapter 8: Puddings and Sweets

FOREWORD

Everything must have a design. This book is a design for cooking, vividly patterned like an enormous patchwork quilt. The design is created from all that is best in Britain in the way of food; and the recipes contained here are the reflections of simple, fulfilling food, made from fresh, home-grown ingredients with old-fashioned recipes that have been favourites for centuries, recipes that have been handed down from generation to generation, recipes from the wide range of nourishing high tea classics and from those lavish breakfasts one now quails to read about.

'Homely' is the word I would use to describe many of the dishes that appear on the following pages and if, to some, 'homely' has a dull sound to it – used, perhaps, to describe plain, rather plump girls – to me it has a warm and comfortable ring, epitomizing the better, more reliable things in life. Here is the sort of food that stands up by itself, made from ingredients good enough to be served as they are rather than being titivated with frills until original flavours are swamped by a flood of other tastes. 'Homely', says the dictionary, is 'intended for home use, simple; without affectation and unpretending.' So are the recipes in this book.

Economy, for most of us, is a vital factor in housekeeping at this time. Fortunately, the British housewife has always been careful in this respect, as these dishes reflect. If one needs to go carefully, then what better place to do it than here. British fishermen, farmers and market gardeners supply us with fresh food all the year round. Unlike most countries we have a twelve-month season with a variety that never ceases to astonish me, and much of it is still very reasonably priced. With the recipes in this book one can live not only cheaply but extremely well.

The recipes cover dishes for every meal; and if you think such homely fare is not smart enough to serve at a dinner party, abandon your prejudices. For years now we have been lulled into the habit of thinking that dinner party food has to be over-sauced and tastelessly pretentious. How much more enjoyable to produce a meal from ingredients so good they need no tarting up. If you must be extravagant when entertaining, forget about creamy sauces into which half a bottle of wine has been poured, and strawberries, flown in from Mexico out of season: settle instead for Scotch smoked salmon, roast sirloin of beef and English hot house peaches. Your success will be far greater and your extravagance will at least be patriotic.

When compiling a book of this kind it is impossible not to leave gaps that may look, to the reader, extraordinary. The line had to be drawn somewhere so, although many of the recipes are old favourites, a great many dishes are those, now often forgotten, which have been tried and enjoyed by my family and friends. As always, I learned while writing. I learned about the use of saffron and was reminded of the qualities of nutmeg; I renewed old friendships with rolled oats and powdered mace; I picked sorrel from the fields and I badgered my butcher to sell me pettitoes (pig's trotters) to serve in a parsley sauce.

Over the centuries we have picked up culinary arts from all those who have travelled across this island, but a basic simplicity and purity prevails in true British cooking. It provides, I feel, something for every taste or occasion; it is this kind of cooking that I have tried to describe and it is this kind of cooking that I am sure you will also enjoy and profit from.

Marika Hanbury Tenison
Maidenwell, March 1975.

There is a tendency to think of stock pots in association with the French, but the British too used to be masters of the art of stock-making. In the days of frugal housekeeping and cool larders our freshly-made farmhouse soups were just as worthy of praise as were any that came from the Continent. It might even be fair to say that, with the exotic influences coming from our distant colonies, we had an even more comprehensive range of flavourings for soups to suit all occasions than our neighbours across the Channel. The use of spices and herbs of all kinds has, for instance, been added to our repertoire of soups made from locally grown ingredients to make them some of the most distinctive in the world.

Bouillabaisse, or fish soup, is also considered to be a prerogative of the French, yet fish soups have been popular around the coasts of Britain for centuries, making cheap and extremely nutritious meals for fishing families and those who live within reach of fresh fish sources. Sadly, this practice seems to have died out in many regions as one of the problems these days, even on the coast, is being able to find a source of fresh fish. If you are very fortunate you may be able to go and stand on the quay at a fishing port when the fishing fleet comes in and buy fresh fish from the fishermen. But all too often their catch is sold almost before it is landed, and much of our best produce from the sea gets sent straight to the continent. Surprisingly, despite modern fishing methods and transport facilities, it is often far harder to buy really fresh fish these days than it was in the days of the horse and carriage when oysters sold at a penny a bushel in London. Now most of our sea harvest is frozen at source – but at least, if we cannot buy the fish still shining with sea water, the British housewife does have access to a wide variety of frozen fish all the year round. And I, for one, would be glad to see those hearty, old-fashioned fish soups coming back into favour.

Delicious soups can be made from almost any combination of fresh fish or shellfish with the addition of an oily fish such as mackerel giving a rich flavour to the brew. Saffron, brought into the west of England by the Phoenicians, helps to give fish soups a special aroma and flavouring.

Methods of Stock-making

The thrifty housewife makes good use of leftovers when making a stock and produces a soup that is far richer and more full of body than one based on the convenient but somehow slightly synthetic-tasting stock cube. Useful these cubes undoubtedly are, but, oh, how bored I am with that particular taste which these days seems to pervade every soup, casserole or stew one samples. Use them in emergencies, certainly; I do frequently, in the same way that I add tomato purée to soups, casseroles and stews when I feel they need extra colour and depth, but use them with care, as too lavish an addition will smother the flavour of the main ingredients and dull the taste buds. Far better results are obtained from a really good home-made stock that relies on the taste of fresh produce rather than synthetic additives.

It is a mistake to make a stock from too many leftover vegetables and too large a combination of ingredients, each smothering the other's taste, but certain things which would otherwise go to waste can give home-made stock a definite life. English cookery books of the eighteenth and nineteenth centuries frequently suggest using herbs and vegetable peelings, especially onion skins, tomato skins and mushroom stalks, in soup cookery. Poultry carcasses make a good, light basic stock; add parsley stalks, celery leaves and a good old-fashioned bouquet garni of marjoram, thyme and bay leaves to give additional flavouring. The addition of small cubes of fried bread gives a crunchy texture that is very pleasant in a bland soup. Another trick I learned in Wales and use often is to add small cubes of Cheddar cheese to a vegetable soup just before it comes to the table; the cheese softens and gives both flavour and texture.

It was really after the First World War, when women in Britain began deserting the kitchen and kitchens began shrinking in size, that the art of stock and soup making gradually began to fall into decline. It wasn't long before the trend became to rely on tinned and then on packet soups, on a stock cube base instead of a home-made stock. Now that the deep freeze is replacing the larder and cool room, fashions are changing again and the home cook can once more begin to create masterpieces from virgin ingredients.

One of the problems inexperienced cooks encounter when making home-made soups and stocks is the fat which almost inevitably rises to the surface of stocks made from a meat or poultry base. This is easily cleared by leaving the stock to settle and then to chill for a few hours. The fat then forms a solid skin above the stock which can be easily removed with a metal cooking spoon dipped in hot water. The fat can later be used as dripping, but care must be taken when frying with it as retained moisture will cause the fat to spit.

Clarifying stock. Cookery is often a series of tricks, and clarifying stock can be simple if you know how. Unless a soup is to be of a thick or puréed variety, it will look far more attractive if the stock has been clarified before the final touches are added. Chill the prepared stock, remove the fat and return the stock to a clean pan. Bring to boiling point, remove from heat and strain through a sieve lined with muslin or through a special felt straining pad (these can be bought from Divertimenti, Marylebone Lane, London W.1).

To make consommé, the stock will have to be more intensely clarified. To do this, first strain the stock, then return to a clean pan with the stiffly beaten whites of 2 eggs and 2 crushed egg shells. Whisk the stock while it boils for about 3 minutes, remove from the heat and leave to settle; then repeat the whisking and settling process three more times. Strain the stock through muslin or felt and you should find it clear and well-coloured. *Note:* Very occasionally this process does not produce a completely clear liquid. If that should happen return the stock to a clean pan, add another whisked egg white and crushed egg shell, and bring to the boil again, whisking all the time. Strain as above.

To thicken soups: Use mashed puréed potato as a thickening instead of a flour and water mixture; *or,* add egg yolks mixed with cream at the last minute and whisk into the soup, heat through but do not boil.

Consommé that is to be served cold must be made from a stock with a jellying ingredient such as poultry bones, a calf's-foot or pork bone, or it will need to have gelatine added.

Root vegetables that are to form the main background of a soup should usually be lightly fried in dripping or oil before the stock is added, to soften them and bring out their flavour. Vegetables such as peas or fresh French beans should never be overcooked. Rich meat soups should be imaginatively seasoned and a good use can be made of wild, natural ingredients such as nettles, sea spinach or sorrel to make fresh-tasting country soups with a difference. A good soup can provide the basis of a nourishing meal for the whole family, an attractive starter for a dinner party, or a pleasant, reviving appetite stimulator for the beginning of a light summer meal.

Additional Notes on Stock-making

Extra flavour can be given to white stocks by adding bacon rinds, by substituting water which has been used for cooking vegetables for cold tap water, or by adding clean peelings from carrots.

For brown stock, extra flavour can be provided by all the above additions as well as by the addition of mushroom peelings, mushroom stalks, tomato and onion skins.

The Use of Stock Cubes in the Twentieth-century Kitchen

People sometimes get the idea that I am against any form of convenience or packaged food. This is not true and indeed I often resort to 'cheating' by using chicken and beef stock cubes – but only in moderation. The taste of stock cubes has a slightly synthetic overtone but in small quantities they will enrich the flavour of a weak stock or soup.

If you have no meat or poultry bones to make stock, I suggest taking the time to peel some onions and root vegetables, combining them with half a stock cube for every pint of water, and simmering the improvised stock for 45–60 minutes.

Keeping Stock

Like most cooked food, stock is particularly susceptible to the action of micro-organisms such as bacteria which can not only cause quick deterioration in the flavour of the stock, but also lead to a potential health hazard. In order to avoid this, stock should always be kept covered in a very cool larder or, preferably, a refrigerator. It should be brought to the boil and quickly cooled at least once every 24 hours for maximum safety.

Stock can be concentrated by fast boiling until reduced by about half. Freeze in ice cube containers and store in a deep freeze for later use.

Making Stock with a Pressure Cooker

Pressure cookers are ideal for stock-making as they preserve all the flavour of the ingredients, make the stock in the shortest possible time and are extremely economical. Follow the instructions for stock-making provided with your pressure cooker.

BASIC STOCK RECIPES

Brown Stock

This makes a really rich and nourishing stock which can be used as the base of many delicious soups, stews, sauces and gravies. It may sound extravagant, but the shin beef can be minced and used to make such things as shepherd's pie, and the stock itself can be kept in a refrigerator for at least four days or frozen in small quantities for use at a later time.

Yield: 6 pints

3 lb shin beef

2 beef marrow bones cut into 2-inch lengths

1 pig's foot (this gives a good jelly consistency)

2 onions

2 carrots

Leaves of 2 celery stalks

2 sprigs parsley

Bouquet garni

10 peppercorns

1 teaspoon salt

6 pints cold water

Cut the meat into 1-inch cubes. Do not peel the onions, but cut them into quarters. Peel and roughly chop the carrot.

Place the meat and bones in a large heavy saucepan. Brown in a hot oven (425° F. Reg. 7), turning every now and then until the meat and bones are a rich brown. Remove from the oven, add the celery leaves, parsley, bouquet garni, peppercorns and salt; add 6 pints water and bring to the boil. Skim off any scum from the surface, return to the boil, cover and simmer very gently for 2 hours. Add the vegetables, bring to the boil again, skim well and continue simmering for a further 2 hours. Strain through a fine sieve and then through muslin or flannel into a large clean bowl. Leave in a refrigerator until the fat has formed a solid layer over the surface. Carefully skim off the fat. *Note:* A similar recipe as this was used up until the early twentieth century for making a concentrated, very strong jelly with a glue-like consistency with a long life that was taken by sailors and soldiers on active service. The stock was boiled and reboiled a number of times, and the final glutinous liquid packed in sterile jars and carefully sealed. When available, fresh vegetables and water were added to reconstitute the soup.

The same method can be used these days, without all the bother of careful preserving, by reducing the strained stock by boiling it without a lid and then freezing the resulting strong stock in ice-cube trays.

Cooked Bone Stock

Use the bones of a chicken or game carcass or the bones from roasted rack of lamb, rib roast of beef, etc., and follow the recipe for a brown stock, chicken or white stock, adding some crumbled commercial stock cube to give additional strength and flavouring.

Chicken Stock

Yield: 6 pints

2 chicken carcasses with giblets
(shop bought cheap bits of chicken
can be used instead)
2 onions
3 carrots

6 peppercorns
1 bay leaf
Bouquet garni
2 leeks (if available)
Salt
6 pints cold water

Break up the carcasses and place them in a large, heavy pan with the peeled onions and carrots, roughly chopped, the leeks, cleaned and chopped, the remaining ingredients, ½ teaspoon salt and the water. Bring slowly to the boil, skim off any scum from the surface, cover and simmer for at least 2½ hours. Strain through a sieve and then through flannel or muslin. Refrigerate until the fat has risen to the surface and set. Remove the fat carefully with a spatula. *Notes:* This stock is adequate in flavour for most requirements. If you wish the flavour to be a little stronger, add ½–1 chicken stock cube. For a really rich chicken consommé that can be served hot or cold, choose a recipe that requires a boiled fowl, e.g. Boiled chicken with mussel sauce. (See page 94.) Cook the chicken in the above stock and strain the enriched liquid through a sieve and then through flannel or muslin. Cool and remove the fat as above. To clarify the stock for a chilled consommé see introductory pages 4–5.

White Meat Stock

Follow the recipe for chicken stock on page 7, substituting lamb or veal bones for the chicken carcass. Add chicken giblets and neck (these can often be bought separately) to give extra flavour.

FAMILY SOUPS

I have included a special section on the soups we have at Maiden-well for lunch on weekdays, because I feel that many people have a budgeting problem these days, and replacing a main course meat dish with a delicious and nourishing rich soup is one way to cut costs while still producing food everyone will enjoy.

We are fortunate enough to produce our own vegetables, but for those who do not have this advantage the vegetables used in this section, provided they are in season, are home-produced and therefore relatively inexpensive. Most of these soups have the addition of a small quantity of meat in some form or other so that they make a meal in themselves. I follow them with fresh fruit or a selection of English cheeses.

The stocks for these soups can be made from stock cubes but, on the whole, it is well worth while making your own in-expensive and nourishing stock at least once a week.

Beef Soup with Forcemeat Balls

Serves 4–5

1 lb shin beef
1 onion
2 carrots
8 oz turnip
1 oz dripping
2 tablespoons flour
2 pints rich beef stock
Salt and freshly ground black pepper
Bouquet garni
1 tablespoon fresh white breadcrumbs
½ tablespoon shredded suet
¼ teaspoon mixed herbs
1 egg
Grated rind of 1 lemon
Salt, pinch cayenne pepper
Pinch nutmeg

Remove any fat from the beef and cut the meat into very small pieces. Peel and very finely chop the onion; peel the carrots and turnip and cut into small dice. Melt the dripping in a heavy pan, add the onion and cook until lightly browned. Remove the onion, add the flour to the juices in the pan and brown quickly over a high heat. Gradually blend in the stock, stirring continually over a high heat until smooth. Add the onions, meat, carrots, turnip and bouquet garni and season with salt and pepper. Bring to the boil, cover and simmer for 1½ hours. Strain the soup.

To make the forcemeat balls, combine the breadcrumbs, suet,

herbs, egg and lemon rind, season with salt, cayenne pepper and a little grated nutmeg and mix well. Form into small balls.

Add the forcemeat balls to the strained soup and cook for a further 30 minutes.

Midsummer Soup

Serves 4–5

3 medium sized carrots
1 onion
1 tablespoon olive oil
1 lb fresh spinach
3 pints stock
8 oz raw gammon
3 pints stock
Salt, pepper and a little ground nutmeg

Peel or scrape and finely chop the carrots. Peel and finely chop the onion. Heat the oil in a large, heavy saucepan and cook the carrots and onion over a low heat, stirring occasionally to prevent sticking until the onion is soft and transparent.

Meanwhile wash the spinach, remove any tough stalks, dry well and chop finely. Finely chop the gammon.

Add the stock to the carrots and onion, bring to the boil, season with salt, pepper and a pinch of ground nutmeg, cover and simmer for 20 minutes. Add the spinach and gammon and cook for a further 15 minutes.

Serve piping hot with crusty, fresh, home-made bread.

Oxtail Soup

Serves 6

1 oxtail
2 onions
2 large carrots
3 sticks celery
1 tablespoon dripping
1 rasher bacon
3 pints beef stock
Bouquet garni and 3 bay leaves

2 tablespoons flour
3 tablespoons water
1 tablespoon Bovril or Marmite
Small glass sherry
Salt and freshly ground black pepper

Ask your butcher to divide the oxtail into joints when you buy it. Soak the tail in cold water for 4 hours or overnight, drain and wipe dry. Peel and roughly chop the onion, peel and chop the carrots and celery. Melt the dripping in a large heavy pan, add the oxtail and brown over a high heat on all sides. Remove oxtail, add the vegetables to the juices in the pan and cook over a medium heat until the onions are golden brown. Add the oxtail, pour in the stock, add the bouquet garni and bay leaves and season with salt and pepper. Bring to the boil, skim off any scum from the surface and simmer for 3 hours or until the meat is falling from the bones. Strain off the stock, cool and refrigerate until the fat has formed a solid skin.

Discard the bouquet garni, bay leaves and vegetables, remove the meat from the bones and shred finely.

Remove the fat from the stock, and heat the stock through. Mix the flour and water to a smooth paste, add to the stock and bring to the boil, stirring all the time. Add the Bovril or Marmite to give colour. Cover and simmer for 3 minutes. Add the meat and sherry, season with salt and pepper and heat through.

Scotch Broth – the Maidenwell way

It is perhaps rather cheeky of me to adapt such a traditional dish as this to suit my own whim. When the authentic Scotch Broth is served, the meat and broth are produced as two separate courses at the same meal. Since they have the same flavouring, I personally find this rather uninteresting. I also feel it is a shame to spoil what, to my mind, is one of the most superb of soups.

In my interpretation, the meat is served in the broth, making an extremely nourishing and hearty soup. Follow it with cheese, salad and fruit and you have the perfect family lunch or supper.

Serves 6

1¼ lb beef skirt
4 pints water

Salt and pepper
1 stock cube
2 carrots
2 onions (or 1 onion and 2 small leeks)
1 turnip
1½ oz pearl barley
Bouquet garni
2 tablespoons finely chopped parsley

Trim the fat off the meat and cut the flesh into small dice. Place the meat, water and stock cubes in a large saucepan, bring to the boil, stir well and remove any scum that rises to the surface. Season, cover and simmer for 1½ hours until the meat is fairly tender.

Peel the carrots and turnip and cut them into small dice. Peel and chop the onion (thinly slice the leeks).

Add the vegetables, pearl barley and bouquet garni to the soup, return to the boil. Cover and simmer for a further 30–45 minutes until the meat, vegetables and barley are all well-cooked. Remove the bouquet garni, add the parsley, check seasoning. Serve very hot with fresh bread.

Chicken Broth with Rice

Serves 4

2 pints rich chicken stock
1 large onion
½ oz butter
3 oz long grain rice
4 oz cooked chicken
1 tablespoon finely chopped chives or spring
onion tops
Salt and pepper

Peel and finely chop the onion. Finely chop the chicken. Heat the butter in a large saucepan, add the onion and cook over a low heat until the onion is soft and transparent. Mix in the rice and stir over a medium low heat until the rice is transparent and all the fat has been absorbed. Add the stock, bring to the boil, season with salt and pepper and cook until the rice is just soft. Mix in the chicken and chives and heat through.

Serve the soup with snippets of fried bread (see page 17).

Cock-a-Leekie Soup

One of those traditional country soups that has nothing synthetic about it and is more of a substantial meal than a soup. Serve it as a main lunch or supper dish and make it the day before it is required so that all the fat can be skimmed from the broth. I use only the breast of the bird for the soup and keep the rest to use in other poultry recipes.

Serves 4

1 boiling fowl (about 2½ lb)
4 fat leeks
2 pints stock (or water and 2½ chicken stock cubes)
1 lb potatoes
Pinch dried tarragon
Salt and freshly ground black pepper
2 tablespoons finely chopped parsley

Remove the giblets from the cavity of the bird. Clean and slice the leeks. Peel the potatoes and cut them into small dice.

Bring the stock to the boil, add the tarragon, seasoning, the chicken (breast down) and the giblets but not the liver. Bring back to the boil, cover and simmer for 40 minutes. Add the leeks and potatoes and continue to simmer slowly for a further 1–1½ hours until the bird is very tender. Remove the chicken from the soup and pour the stock and vegetables into a bowl. Chill overnight.

Cut the breast of the chicken into small dice. Skim off all the fat from the stock and return the stock and vegetables to a clean pan. Add the diced chicken and the parsley. Heat through and check seasoning before serving.

Thick Country Chicken Soup

Serves 4

2 pints good chicken stock
8 oz mashed potatoes
4 oz cooked chicken
2 tablespoons finely chopped parsley
Salt and freshly ground black pepper

Chop the chicken very finely. Heat the chicken stock and add a
¼ pint to the mashed potatoes. Mix to a smooth paste and add the
remaining stock. Heat the soup in a saucepan until just boiling and
strain through a fine sieve to remove any lumps. Return to a clean
pan, add the chicken and parsley, season with salt and pepper and
simmer for 10 minutes.

Serve the soup with small croutons of fried bread (see page 17).

FARMHOUSE VEGETABLE SOUPS

Vegetable soups made with fresh seasonal vegetables make the
most delicious and nourishing dishes. During the week at
Maidenwell, there are nearly always eight or more of us for
lunch, and about a year ago I began having a vegetable soup
instead of a meat dish at least every other day. It was an instant
success; everyone enjoyed the soup and since then we have stuck
to a happy routine of soup and cheese lunches with the soup varying according to what vegetables were in season and served with
thick slices of home-made bread.

The variations, of course, are infinite. A good home-made stock
helps to provide flavour but if that is not available chicken or beef
stock cubes (I much prefer those made by Knorr) can be used
instead. All the vegetables except those for a puréed soup should
be *finely* chopped and extra taste can be incorporated by the careful use of herbs and spices.

A hearty soup served as a main course for lunch or supper
makes an economical and satisfactory meal. Both varieties can
also be served before a light main course, but care should be
taken to ensure that purées are not too thick: thick purée can
be thinned by adding additional stock or milk.

Bountiful Soup

Serves 6

1 *medium-sized potato*
1 *large carrot*
2 *leeks*

1 tablespoon olive oil or ½ oz butter
1 large tin tomatoes (14 oz)
1 Cox's apple
1¼ pints water
½ teaspoon curry powder
Juice 1 orange
Salt and pepper
2 tablespoons finely chopped parsley

Peel and dice the potato. Peel and dice the carrot. Remove the tough green leaves of the leeks and slice the tender shoots. Peel and dice the apple.

Heat the oil or butter, add the potato, carrot and leeks and cook over a low heat, stirring to prevent sticking. Add the tomatoes, apple, water, curry powder and orange juice, season with salt and pepper, bring to the boil, cover and simmer for 30 minutes or until all the vegetables are tender. Purée through a fine sieve, a food mill or a liquidizer, return to a clean pan, check seasoning and garnish with chopped parsley just before serving.

Chestnut Soup

Look in any park land in this country and you will probably find half a dozen or more chestnut trees, the eating kind, not the purely decorative conker variety. They were grown not only for their attractive appearance but also for the richness of their fruit, and chestnuts used to be popular in many soup, vegetable and force-meat recipes. Chestnut soup is a rich warming starter.

Serves 4–5

1 lb chestnuts
1 onion
½ oz butter
1 pint chicken stock
1 pint milk
Salt, pepper and a pinch of cayenne
¼ pint single cream

Make a cross with a sharp knife across the top of the chestnuts. Cover them with water, bring to the boil and boil for about 30 minutes until the chestnuts are quite tender. Drain off the water and leave the chestnuts to stand until cool enough to handle. Remove the shells and outer skins of the chestnuts.

Peel and finely chop the onion. Heat the butter in a saucepan, add the onion and cook over a medium heat until the onion is soft and transparent. Add the chestnuts and pour over the stock and milk. Bring to the boil, cover and simmer until the chestnuts are mushy, about 20 minutes. Purée through a sieve, a food mill or in an electric liquidizer and return to a clean pan. Heat through, season with salt, pepper and a pinch of cayenne and blend in the cream just before serving.

Chicken and Celery Soup

Chicken and celery make excellent partners and this is an ideal way of using up small amounts of cooked chicken.

Serves 4

4 sticks celery

1 onion

8 oz cooked chicken

1 oz butter

1 tablespoon flour

2 pints chicken stock (or water and stock cube)

Pinch marjoram and basil

Salt and pepper

2 egg yolks

3 tablespoons double cream

Chop the celery finely. Peel and finely chop the onion. Cut the chicken into small dice. Melt the butter, add the onion and celery and cook over a low heat until the vegetables are soft and transparent. Add the flour, mix well and gradually blend in the stock, stirring continually until the sauce is smooth. Add the herbs, season with salt and pepper, bring to the boil, cover and simmer until the vegetables are tender.

Beat together the egg yolks and the cream and beat them into the soup, taking care not to let the liquid boil. Add the chicken, heat through, check seasoning and serve at once.

Curried Apple and Turnip Soup

Can be served either hot or cold and has an unusual piquant flavour. Use the winter rather than the small white turnips.

Serves 4–5

3 cooking apples
1 onion
12 oz turnip
½ oz butter
1 teaspoon curry paste
2 pints good chicken or white stock
Salt and pepper

Peel and roughly chop the apples, turnip and onion.

Melt the butter in a large saucepan. Add the onion and turnip and cook over a low heat until the onion is transparent and most of the fat has been absorbed. Add the apple and continue to cook over a low heat for a further 3 minutes, stirring to prevent sticking or browning. Mix in the curry paste and add the stock.

Bring to the boil, cover and simmer for about 30 minutes or until the turnip is absolutely tender. Liquidize the soup or purée it through a fine sieve or food mill and return to a clean pan. Heat through and adjust for seasoning. *Note:* Hot soup can be served with small snippets of fried bread – see below. Cold soup can be served with a spoonful of sour cream or fresh cream flavoured with lemon juice, salt and pepper.

Snippets of Fried Bread to Serve with Soup

Enough for 4

2 thin slices of white bread
Lard for frying

Remove the crusts from the bread and cut slices into thin diagonal strips and then into small triangles or diamond shapes. Fry until golden brown and crisp in hot lard and drain on kitchen paper. Serve in a bowl to accompany a hot or cold soup.

Garden Pea Soup

Like so many traditional recipes this is best kept as simple and plain as possible, especially if it is to be made, as it should be, with small, bright green garden peas.

Serves 4–5

1 lb small fresh or frozen peas
1 shallot or small onion
1 pint milk
½ pint chicken stock
Salt, pepper and ¼ teaspoon sugar
4 leaves fresh mint
¼ pint cream
2 leaves fresh mint for garnish

Peel and very finely chop the shallot or onion. Combine the peas, shallot, chicken stock, milk, seasoning, sugar, and the 4 mint leaves in a saucepan, bring to the boil and simmer for 5–15 minutes until the peas are very soft. Remove the mint and purée through a sieve, a food mill or in an electric liquidizer and return to a clean pan. Heat through, check the seasoning, blend in the cream and serve at once with a garnish of finely chopped fresh mint leaves.

Croutons of fried bread can also be served with the soup.

Jellied Cucumber Soup

Serves 4

2 pints clear stock
1½ packets gelatine (¾ oz)
1 large cucumber
Juice 1 lemon
1 tablespoon dry sherry
4 tablespoons double cream
Salt and white pepper
4 leaves fresh mint, finely chopped

Pass the stock through a very fine sieve. Chill in a refrigerator and remove every particle of fat from the surface. Combine 4 tablespoonfuls stock with the gelatine powder in a small saucepan and heat over a low heat, stirring continually until the gelatine has melted. Add half the lemon juice and the sherry and mix with the stock. Season with salt and pepper and chill until the soup is lightly jelled.

Peel the cucumber and coarsely grate the flesh. Combine the cream with the rest of the lemon juice and season lightly with salt and pepper. Mix the cucumber into the jellied soup using a fork or a wire whisk and spoon the soup into 4 chilled bowls. Top each bowl with a dollop of the cream and garnish with the chopped mint leaves. *Notes:* Tinned consommé can be used for this soup but in that case the gelatine should be omitted. A drop or two of green food colouring can be added to the stock but be very sparing or the soup will quickly become an unnatural and unappetizing colour.

June Soup

Serves 6

> 8 oz carrots
> 1 large onion
> 1 oz dripping or butter
> 1 lb new potatoes
> ¾ lb courgettes or young marrow, sliced
> 3 pints good stock
> Salt and freshly ground black pepper

Peel the carrots and cut them into small dice. Peel and chop the onion. Scrape the potatoes and cut them into small dice.

Heat the dripping or butter in a large heavy pan. Add the onion and carrots and cook over a low heat, stirring to prevent browning, for 5 minutes. Add the courgettes and the stock, season with salt and pepper, bring to the boil, cover and simmer for 15 minutes or until the carrots and potatoes are tender.

Pea and Sorrel Soup

Sorrel is a flavouring and salad ingredient that used to be popular in English cookery but is sadly all too seldom seen these days. However, it does grow wild in many of our fields and can easily be cultivated in even the smallest garden. The flavour is fabulous so it is well worth taking the trouble to get hold of some.

Serves 6

> 1 onion
> 1 tablespoon olive oil
> 1 bunch sorrel (about 12 large leaves)

2½ pints light stock (or water
and 2 chicken stock cubes)
1 lb fresh or frozen peas
Peel of 1 lemon, grated
Salt and freshly ground black pepper

Peel and finely chop the onion, wash the sorrel leaves and pat dry with kitchen paper.

Heat the oil in a large saucepan, add the onion and cook over a low heat until the onion is soft and transparent. Add the sorrel leaves and stir with a wooden spoon until they are soft and limp. Add the stock and bring to the boil. Add the peas, return to the boil, season with salt and pepper, cover and simmer for about 8–15 minutes until the peas are just tender. Purée the soup through a fine sieve, through a food mill or in an electric liquidizer. Return to a clean pan, heat through, add lemon peel and check seasoning.

Potato, Celery and Cheese Soup

Serves 4

1 lb old potatoes
4 large sticks celery
2 medium-sized onions
1 oz butter
1 pint light stock (or water
and 1½ chicken stock cubes)
¼ pint milk
2 tablespoons cream
Salt and white pepper
2 oz Cheddar cheese

Peel and roughly chop the potatoes. Remove the leaves of the celery sticks and chop the stalks into ½-inch pieces. Peel and chop the onions.

Melt the butter in a large, heavy pan. Add the celery and onion and cook over a low heat until the onion is soft and transparent. Add the potatoes and stock and season with salt and pepper. Bring to the boil and simmer for 20–30 minutes until the potatoes and celery are tender. Purée through a sieve, a food mill or in an electric liquidizer. Return to a clean pan, add the milk, re-heat, stir in the cream and check the seasoning. Pour into well-heated bowls and sprinkle with grated cheese.

Potato and Turnip Soup

Serves 4

$\frac{3}{4}$ *lb potatoes*
1 large turnip
1 small onion
$\frac{3}{4}$ *pint chicken or white stock*
1$\frac{1}{2}$ pints milk
2 bay leaves
Pinch mixed herbs
Salt and pepper
1 tablespoon finely chopped parsley

Peel and roughly chop the potatoes, turnip and onion. Combine the potatoes, turnip, onion and herbs in a heavy saucepan with the stock. Bring to the boil and simmer gently for about 30 minutes or until the vegetables are soft. Remove the bay leaves, leave to cool a little and then purée through a fine sieve, in an electric liquidizer or a food mill. Return the purée to a clean pan, add the milk, season with salt and pepper. Heat through, mix in the chopped parsley and serve at once.

Winter Soup

Serves 6

$\frac{1}{2}$ *lb potatoes*
$\frac{1}{2}$ *lb carrots*
$\frac{1}{2}$ *lb onions*
$\frac{1}{2}$ *lb turnip*
4 oz parsnip
4 oz swede
1 oz butter
1$\frac{1}{2}$ pints chicken stock
1 oz flour
1 pint milk
Salt and white pepper
2 oz Cheddar cheese

Peel and finely chop the onions. Peel the other vegetables and cut them into small dice.

Melt the butter in a heavy saucepan, add all the vegetables and cook them over a medium heat until the onions are transparent – shake the pan frequently to prevent sticking or burning. Pour over the stock, season generously with salt and pepper, bring to the boil, cover and simmer for about 20 minutes or until the vegetables are tender. Add a little of the milk to the flour and stir into a smooth paste. Add the paste to the soup with the rest of the milk and stir well until the soup thickens slightly. Bring to the boil and simmer for a further 5 minutes. Taste for seasoning, mix in the grated cheese and serve at once.

CREAMED SOUPS

Brussels Sprout and Almond Soup

Serves 6

½ lb Brussels sprouts
1½ oz ground almonds
3½ pints white stock
4 bay leaves
Salt and freshly ground pepper
½ pint single cream
2 oz split blanched almonds

Peel off the tough outer leaves of the sprouts. Combine the sprouts with the almonds and stock, add the bay leaves and seasoning, bring to the boil and simmer for 30 minutes. Purée the soup through a fine sieve, a food mill or in an electric liquidizer until it has the consistency of velvet and return it to a clean saucepan. Add the cream, heat through without boiling and check seasoning. Roast the split, blanched almonds in a hot oven until golden and serve the soup with a garnish of roast almonds.

Cream of Cauliflower Soup with Prawns

Serves 5–6

1 small cauliflower
1 small onion
1 stick celery
½ oz butter

1 tablespoon flour
2 pints chicken stock
¼ pint single cream
Salt, white pepper and a pinch of nutmeg
4 oz peeled prawns
1 tablespoon finely chopped parsley

Remove the outer leaves and tough stem of the cauliflower and
steam the head over boiling water for 20–30 minutes until very
tender.

Peel and finely chop the onion. Remove the leaves and finely
chop the celery stick. Melt the butter, add the onion and celery
and cook over a medium heat, stirring to prevent sticking, until the
onion is soft and transparent. Add the flour and mix well. Gradually add the stock, stirring continually over a medium high heat
until smooth. Bring to the boil, add the cauliflower and simmer for
2 minutes. Purée through a fine sieve, a food mill or in an electric
liquidizer and return to a clean pan. Add the cream, season with
salt, pepper and nutmeg, stir in the prawns and heat through.
Serve at once with a garnish of finely chopped parsley.

Cream of Celery Soup

By browning the grated cheese on top of the soup under a hot
grill just before serving you can create an interesting combination
of textures and flavours.

Serves 4–5

1 lb potatoes
1 large onion
1 head celery
1½ oz butter
1 pint chicken stock
1 pint milk
Salt and freshly ground black pepper
¼ pint single cream
2 oz finely grated Cheddar cheese
Little cayenne pepper

Peel and dice the potatoes. Peel and chop the onion. Wash and
finely chop the stalks and leaves of the celery including the thick
white base.

Melt the butter in a large, heavy saucepan, add the vegetables and cook over a medium heat, stirring to prevent sticking, until the onion is soft and transparent. Add the stock, bring to the boil, blend in the milk and simmer for 45 minutes until the vegetables are really tender. Purée the soup through a fine sieve, a food mill or in an electric liquidizer and return to a clean pan. Add the cream, season with salt and pepper, heat through and pour into earthenware bowls. Sprinkle the cheese on the surface, top with a small pinch of cayenne pepper and cook under a hot grill until the cheese has melted and is golden. Serve at once with hot, crusty bread.

Cream of Mushroom Soup

This soup is quite unlike tinned mushroom soups and even better if made with fresh field mushrooms – although then the colour is inclined to be a little on the grey side. (This is unavoidable, but the appearance can be improved by a lavish sprinkling of chopped parsley before serving.)

Serves 4–5

¼ lb firm mushrooms
1 oz butter
1 tablespoon flour
1 pint chicken stock
¼ pint milk
¼ pint cream
Salt and white pepper
Pinch nutmeg

Thinly slice the mushrooms. Melt the butter in a heavy saucepan. Add the mushrooms and cook over a low heat for 3 minutes, stirring to prevent sticking or browning. Add the flour and mix lightly. Gradually add the stock, stirring continually over a medium heat until the soup comes to the boil and is completely smooth. Blend in the milk, season with salt, pepper and nutmeg and simmer for 10 minutes. Add the cream and heat through. Serve at once.

Cream of Parsnip and Potato Soup

One of those delicious, satiny cream soups that really delight the palate with their unadulterated flavour.

Serves 4

¾ lb parsnips
2 medium-sized potatoes
1 large onion
Juice of ½ lemon
1 pint white stock (or
1 pint water and 1 chicken stock cube)
1 pint milk
Salt, pepper and ¼ teaspoon ground nutmeg
1 tablespoon finely chopped parsley

Peel and roughly chop the parsnips, potatoes and onion.

Combine the vegetables and lemon juice in a pan with enough cold water to cover them. Season with a little salt, bring to the boil and simmer for 15–20 minutes until the vegetables are tender. Purée the vegetables with the liquid they have been cooked in through a fine sieve, a food mill or in an electric liquidizer. Return the purée of vegetables to a clean pan, add the milk and stock, season with freshly ground black pepper and nutmeg and bring slowly to the boil, stirring continuously. Reduce the heat, simmer slowly for 10 minutes, check seasoning, mix in the finely chopped parsley and serve at once with a garnish of small snippets of fried bread.

Watercress and Potato Soup

Serves 6

2 bunches watercress
1 lb potatoes
1 small onion or shallot
1 oz butter
1 tablespoon flour
2 pints chicken stock
Salt, pepper and a pinch nutmeg
¼ pint cream

Wash and roughly chop the watercress, putting aside a few leaves for garnish. Peel and dice the potatoes. Peel and chop the onion or shallot.

Melt the butter in a heavy saucepan, add the onion and cook over a low heat for 2 minutes until the onion is soft. Add the flour and mix well. Add the stock, stirring continually over a medium high heat until the soup comes to the boil and is smooth. Add the watercress and potatoes, season with salt, pepper and nutmeg and simmer for 30 minutes or until the potato is tender. Purée the soup through a fine sieve, a food mill or in an electric liquidizer and return to a clean pan. Re-heat, blend in the cream and add the remaining watercress, finely chopped.

FISH SOUPS

Cream of Haddock Soup with Prawns

Serves 4

1 pint fish or chicken stock
1 lb smoked haddock
1 onion
$\frac{3}{4}$ pint milk
$\frac{1}{4}$ pint double cream
Salt and freshly ground black pepper
1 tablespoon finely chopped parsley
3–4 oz peeled prawns

Place the fish in a shallow dish, skin side up, and pour over enough boiling water to cover. Peel off the skin, remove any bones and roughly chop the flesh.

Peel and finely chop the onion. Place the onion and haddock in a heavy pan, pour over the stock, bring to the boil and simmer for about 30 minutes or until the haddock is very tender. Purée the fish through a sieve, a food mill or in an electric liquidizer and return to a clean pan. Add the milk, heat through, season with salt and pepper (be sparing with the salt as the haddock is salty anyway) and blend in the cream. Pour into bowls and garnish with a few prawns and a little finely chopped parsley. Serve hot or well chilled.

Fresh Fish Soup

Fresh fish is one of the greatest pleasures of this island – this soup
makes a delicious first course or supper dish.

Serves 4

1 lb fresh haddock

1 onion

3 carrots

6 peppercorns

8 shallots

2 potatoes

1 oz butter

1 tablespoon flour

$\frac{1}{4}$ pint single cream

1 stock cube

2 bay leaves

1 sprig thyme

2 sage leaves

Salt and pepper

Pinch nutmeg

2 tablespoons finely chopped parsley

Place the haddock in a pan with 1 onion, peeled and sliced, 1 carrot
roughly chopped, the bay leaves, thyme and sage, the peppercorns
and a little salt. Cover with water, bring to the boil and simmer
gently for about 10 minutes until the fish is just tender. Remove
the haddock, skin the fish, take out all the bones and flake the flesh.
Strain the liquid the fish was cooked in and add enough water to
make 2 pints.

Peel and dice the potatoes. Peel and dice remaining carrots and
peel the shallots. Melt the butter in a saucepan, add the vegetables
and cook over a low heat without browning for 5 minutes. Add the
flour, mix lightly and gradually blend in the liquid, stirring continually until smooth. Bring to the boil, add the stock cube, and
simmer for 15–20 minutes until the vegetables are tender.

Add the fish, nutmeg, cream and parsley. Season, heat through
without boiling and serve at once.

Mackerel Broth

Mackerel has had a strange history in this country. For centuries many townspeople have believed mackerel to be a dirty feeder and have treated it with disdain; yet this fish, to my way of thinking, is one of the richest and most delicious of those caught around our shores. Being plentiful it is also inexpensive, even in these days, and a relatively small quantity of fish can provide a surprisingly satisfying meal. In the West Country, particularly, you find a wide selection of mackerel dishes from plain grilled to those that are smoked in small factories along the coast and which are infinitely superior to the more expensive smoked trout.

How you prepare and cook your mackerel is a matter of taste, but you cannot go far wrong by making them into a delicious and aromatic soup; more than a first course and almost a meal in its own right. Served with hunks of crusty bread and farmhouse butter they make an attractive, cheap and exceptionally nourishing dish.

Serves 4

1 mackerel filleted
2 pints chicken stock
2 tablespoons finely chopped parsley
1 teaspoon lemon juice
Salt, pepper and a pinch cayenne

Cut the mackerel fillets into thin strips about a $\frac{1}{4}$ inch wide and 1 inch long. Heat the chicken stock until boiling.

Arrange the strips of mackerel in the bottom of a clean saucepan, pour over the boiling stock and simmer for about 5 minutes or until the fish is just tender. Add the parsley, lemon juice and seasoning and serve at once with hot crusty bread.

Charlestown Mackerel Soup

Serves 6

4 small mackerel
Flour
1 large potato

2 leeks
1 clove garlic
1 oz butter
2 bay leaves
1 tin tomatoes (15 oz)
1½ pints milk
1 tin mussels in brine
1 teaspoon saffron
Salt and freshly ground black pepper

Remove the heads and tails of the mackerel and clean the fish. Cut each fish into pieces about 2 inches thick and dust lightly with flour seasoned with salt, pepper and just a tiny pinch of cayenne.

Peel the potato and cut into very small dice. Clean and slice the leeks. Peel and finely chop the garlic. Soak the saffron in 2 table-spoons boiling water. Melt the butter in a heavy saucepan. Add the potato, garlic and leeks and cook over a low heat, shaking the pan to prevent sticking, for about 10 minutes or until the potato is beginning to soften. Add the mackerel and cook over a medium heat for 3 minutes, turning the fish every now and then. Add the tomatoes, broken up with a fork, and the bay leaves and simmer for a further 10 minutes. Blend in the milk, mussels and liquid and the strained liquid from the saffron, season with salt and pepper and simmer for a final 5 minutes. Remove bay leaves, season and serve at once with garlic bread.

Queen or Scallop Broth with Saffron

Smaller than scallops, and very much less expensive, queens seldom seem to be found outside Cornwall, Devon and the north-west coast of Scotland. Their flavour is delicate and their texture superb.

Serves 4

¾ pint queens or 6 scallops
1 small onion
2 leeks
2 medium-sized potatoes
½ oz butter
1½ pints chicken stock

Salt and pepper
½ teaspoon strand saffron
1 tablespoon chopped parsley
¼ pint single cream

Peel and finely chop the onion. Clean and thinly slice leeks. Peel the potatoes and cut them into small dice.

Melt the butter in a heavy pan. Add the vegetables, season with salt and pepper and cook over a low heat, stirring continually until the leeks and onion are soft and transparent and the butter is absorbed. Add the stock, bring to the boil and simmer for 20 minutes or until potatoes are cooked. Cool and purée in an electric liquidizer, through a food mill or a fine sieve. Return the soup to a clean pan.

Soak the saffon in 1 tablespoon boiling water for 5 minutes and strain through a fine sieve. Remove any black veins from the sides of the queens and separate the pink coral from the body. Cut the queens in half. Heat the soup to boiling point and drop in the queens. Add saffron water, lower the heat and cook gently for 3 minutes. Add cream, stirring continuously, check seasoning and serve in heated bowls with a little chopped parsley on the surface.

2
Fish

From the magnificent salmon to the humble sprat: the wealth of our sea waters is almost as great as that of our farming land, with a vast range of marine life that can provide dishes of high nutritional value as well as varied taste.

Deep freezing has brought the deep sea running fish to our kitchens in first-class condition; recently developed methods of even deeper fishing are giving us new types of fish for the table; hopefully, less expensive farmed oysters and shellfish will be with us before too long. On the other hand, freezing has also given us such horrors as the 'fish finger' – so that for many people the word 'fish' is associated with a piece of tasteless blotting-paper, oblong shaped, with a coating of synthetic orange-coloured crumbs.

The taste of almost any fresh fish is superb if it is properly cooked. Freshness is vital where fish is concerned, except, perhaps in the case of salmon which can, if it is not to be cooked straight from the river, be hung like meat. I found this recommended in one ancient English cookery book and tried it with interesting results; the taste was different but not in the least unacceptable and extremely rich. Fish should be chosen with care and bought when the scales are still shining and the eyes bright; the shells of lobsters should be pliable and the tail coiled so that it springs back into shape if you pull it straight, and other shellfish should have a fresh smell of salt water and ozone to them. A dull glazed look should be avoided at all costs when buying fish of any kind.

One of the disadvantages of buying fish from a fishmonger is that it may have been frozen and, like all frozen food, it will deteriorate more quickly than a fresh product. It must, therefore, be used within 24 hours of thawing. A good fishmonger should answer you honestly when you ask if fish has been frozen or not; if he is not an honest man, find another fishmonger.

In Cornwall where I live, we are perhaps particularly blessed with fresh produce from the sea, and it is still possible to find fresh cockles in their shells, freshly boiled crabs, queens (small scallops) and even squid for sale. We also get some of the fish more commonly associated with the Mediterranean, such as red mullet, gurnard and John Dory. I find the answer to most people's cry of 'Oh, but I never find anything like that in my local fish-monger' is that they don't ask for it. The fishmonger, like every-one else, is a victim of the supply and demand syndrome; fish is relatively inexpensive compared to meat and we the housewives are at fault if we don't get the variety we would like. Demand, search and, if necessary, nag, and in the end you will get results.

We have become a nation of meat eaters, and we are missing a lot and wasting money. I would like to see every family have at least four meatless, fish-based dishes a week, as indeed people did when oysters were one penny a dozen and somebody died of a surfeit of lampreys.

Most fish benefit from the complement of a sauce as most meats benefit from the complement of a bit of gravy, and these sauces need to be light, subtle and flavoured to partner the texture and flavour of the fish. Most of our sauces have their background in ideas imported from other lands, but some traditionally British ones still remain favourites: sauces like egg, mustard and parsley which in no way detract from the basic flavour of the fish but indeed help to bring it out.

Never, in your search for good food, overlook the possibilities of the more mundane seafood like cockles, the small whitebait or the unassuming sprat. They can make dishes exciting enough to serve at the most sophisticated dinner party and the nutritional value of the common herring, for instance, is enormous.

COD

Codling Pie

I found the original recipe for this in an eighteenth-century cookery book. In that edition the pie had a pastry crust, but since potatoes were included in the ingredients, I have substituted an extra layer of potatoes browned to a crusty deliciousness in place of the heavier, more starchy topping.

Serves 6

$\frac{3}{4}$ lb cod fillet
2 hard-boiled eggs

1½ lb potatoes
2 large onions
1 teaspoon made mustard
4 anchovy fillets
½ teaspoon Worcestershire sauce
¼ pint water
2 oz butter
Freshly ground black pepper

Steam the cod for about 10 minutes over boiling water. Remove the skin and coarsely flake the flesh.

Shell and roughly chop the hard-boiled eggs. Peel and very thinly slice the potatoes and onions and separate into rings. Finely chop the anchovies. Make a sauce by combining the mustard, anchovies, Worcestershire sauce and water, season with pepper and mix well.

Well grease a shallow baking dish and arrange thin layers of potatoes, onions, eggs and fish, seasoning each layer with a little of the sauce and finishing with a fairly thick layer of potatoes. Dot 2 oz butter in very small pieces over the surface and sprinkle the top with a little extra freshly ground black pepper. Bake the pie in a moderate oven (350° F. Reg. 4) for 45–60 minutes until the potatoes are cooked and the topping is a crisp golden brown.

Fisherman's Pie

Serves 4

1lb fresh cod, haddock or coley, filleted
2½ oz butter
Juice ½ lemon
2 hard-boiled eggs
4 oz frozen peas
2 tablespoons finely chopped parsley
1 lb potatoes
¾ pint milk
3 tablespoons double cream
1½ oz grated Cheddar cheese
Salt and freshly ground black pepper
2 tablespoons flour
1 small onion
Bouquet garni
6 peppercorns

Place the fish in a fireproof dish, dot with 1½ oz butter and pour over the lemon juice. Cover with tinfoil or greaseproof paper and cook in a moderate oven (350° F. Reg. 4) for 20 minutes. Remove any skin or bones and flake the fish, reserving the juices.

Peel the potatoes and boil until soft. Drain well and mash until smooth with the cream and ½ oz butter. Season with salt and pepper.

Cook the peas in boiling salted water until just tender. Combine the milk, onion (peeled), bouquet garni and peppercorns in a saucepan, bring to the boil and simmer gently for 2 minutes. Strain.

Heat ½ oz butter in a clean pan, add the flour and mix well. Gradually blend in the milk, stirring continually until the sauce comes to the boil and is thick and smooth. Blend in 1 oz cheese and season with salt and pepper.

Chop the hard-boiled eggs. Fold the fish, juice, parsley, eggs and peas into the sauce and transfer to a lightly greased pie dish. Spread mashed potato over the top, sprinkle with the remaining cheese and heat through in a hot oven (425° F. Reg. 7) until the cheese topping is bubbling and golden brown.

West Coast Fish Stew

An old-fashioned recipe similar to the French *Bouillabaisse* that is extremely rich and nourishing. It should be served in deep soup plates and accompanied by thick slices of fresh crusty bread.

Serves 4

1¼ lb fresh cod fillet
Flour
Cayenne
2 sticks celery
1 onion
2 leeks
2 carrots
2 cloves garlic
6 small ripe tomatoes
1 tablespoon tomato purée
2 anchovy fillets

1 teaspoon capers
2 bay leaves
Pinch thyme and sage
1½ pints chicken or fish stock
4 tablespoons olive oil
Salt and freshly ground black pepper
Pinch saffron soaked in 1 tablespoon boiling water

Cut the fish into pieces roughly 2 inches square. Roll the fish pieces in flour seasoned with salt and a little cayenne pepper. Heat the oil in a saucepan until smoking. Add the fish and cook quickly over a high heat until the fish is crisp and golden brown on both sides. Remove from the pan with a slotted spoon and drain off excess fat on kitchen paper. Leave the fish on one side. Strain remaining oil into a saucepan.

Peel and thinly slice celery and onion. Clean and thinly slice leeks. Peel and thinly slice carrots. Peel and crush garlic cloves. Peel tomatoes (see page 128), remove the cores and roughly chop the flesh.

Heat the oil in the saucepan, add celery, onion, leeks and carrots and cook over a low heat until onions are soft and transparent. Add tomatoes, tomato purée, anchovies, roughly chopped, the capers, and herbs (except saffron), mix well. Add the stock, season with salt and pepper and bring to the boil. Cover and simmer gently for 5 minutes. Strain off the saffron juice and add to the stew for the last 5 minutes of cooking time. Place the fried fish in the bottom of a large heated serving dish. Pour over the very hot stew and serve at once.

Striplets of Cod in Batter

The batter used in this recipe is so light that it melts rather than cloys in the mouth and so crisp it will remain satisfyingly crunchy for a surprising length of time.

Serves 4

1 lb cod or white fish fillet
Deep fat or oil for frying
4 oz flour
3 tablespoons olive oil

Pinch of salt
8 fluid oz water
1 egg white

Remove any bones from the cod fillet and place it skin side down on a board. Using a sharp knife, cut the fillet lengthwise into finger-sized strips about ¼ inch wide. Cut the strips into 2-inch lengths.

Mix the olive oil with the flour and salt and blend in the water. Whisk the batter until smooth with a wire whisk and leave it to stand for 30 minutes. Whisk the egg white stiff and fold lightly into the batter. Dip the cod striplets into the batter and fry them in very hot deep fat or oil until crisp and a light golden brown. Drain on kitchen paper and serve with tartare sauce.

HADDOCK

Cullen Skink

Not the most romantic sounding name but nevertheless a delicious soup. Its name comes from the Scottish words *cullen*, a fish, and *skink*, a stew-like soup (or a soup-like stew). Traditionally it should be made with Finnan haddock but if this is not available the ordinary kind will do.

Serves 4

1 lb smoked haddock fillets
½ lb mashed potatoes
½ lb young leeks
1 pint chicken or fish stock
¼ pint dry white wine
½ pint single cream
1 egg yolk
Salt and pepper

Place the haddock fillets in a heavy saucepan, pour over the stock, bring to the boil and simmer gently for 10 minutes until the fish is just tender. Pour off and reserve the stock. Skin and bone the fish and cut the fillets into 1-inch pieces.

Wash and trim the leeks and very finely slice the flesh. Combine the stock and potatoes in a clean pan, bring to the boil, simmer for 5 minutes and rub through a sieve. Combine the sieved liquid with the leeks, bring to the boil and cook for 10 minutes or until the leeks are tender. Add the fish and wine, season with salt and pepper, and cook for a further 5 minutes. Blend in the cream and egg yolk and serve at once. A little finely chopped leeks can be kept back from the recipe and used as a garnish, added just before serving.

Finnan Haddock Soufflé

Serves 6

2 Finnan haddocks
$\frac{1}{4}$ pint milk
$\frac{1}{2}$ oz butter
White pepper
1 oz butter
1 oz flour
3 eggs
Salt and pepper

Arrange the haddocks in a pan with $\frac{1}{4}$ pint milk and $\frac{1}{2}$ oz butter. Season with pepper, bring to the boil and simmer gently for about 15 minutes or until the haddock is tender. Strain off and reserve the milk and leave the haddock to cool. Remove all the skin and bones from the fish and flake the flesh with a fork.

Melt 1 oz butter in a saucepan, add the flour and mix well. Gradually blend in the milk the haddock was cooked in, stirring continuously until the mixture is thick and smooth.

Separate the eggs and beat the yolks until smooth and beat them into the soufflé base. Lightly mix in the haddock and season with just a little pinch of salt and some pepper.

Beat the egg whites until they are stiff and light but not dry – they should stand in peaks. Fold them into the soufflé mixture and transfer to a lightly greased soufflé dish. Bake in a hot oven (400° F. Reg. 6) for about 35 minutes until the soufflé is well risen and just beginning to crack on the surface.

Golden Haddock with Prawns

A deliciously simple but sophisticated dish. It must be served as soon as it is ready, although the preparation can be done in advance.

Serves 4

1½ *lb smoked haddock fillets*
½ *pint milk*
¼ *pint double cream*
½ *oz butter*
1 *tablespoon flour*
1½ *oz grated Cheddar cheese*
4 *oz prawns*
Salt, pepper and cayenne
4 *eggs*

Arrange the fish fillets in a deep frying pan. Pour over the milk and cream, bring to the boil and simmer gently for about 10 minutes until the fish is tender. Drain off and reserve the juices and skin the haddock, removing any bones. Arrange the haddock in a lightly greased, shallow fireproof serving dish. Strain the juices from the pan through a sieve and reserve.

Poach the eggs in boiling water until just soft. Slide out on a perforated spoon on to a plate and trim off any untidy edges with kitchen scissors. Place the poached eggs on the haddock.

Melt the butter in a saucepan, add the flour and mix well. Gradually add the liquor from the cooked fish, stirring continually over a low heat until the sauce is thick and smooth – do not boil. Add the cheese and continue to cook until the cheese has melted. Add prawns. Season the sauce with salt and pepper and pour it over the eggs. Sprinkle with a little cayenne and brown under a hot grill until the top of the dish is a golden brown and the fish is hot through.

Haddock Kedgeree

Although originally a breakfast dish, kedgeree is a little too heady for most people to tackle first thing in the morning these days, so serve it for lunch or as a supper dish when you want something that is simple but delicious. If you have weekend guests, resurrect it as a late Sunday breakfast, and if you happen to be giving a late party and plan to serve an early morning snack with coffee before the guests leave, then kedgeree is a must.

The secret of good kedgeree is to add raw eggs and some cream at the last minute and to serve it immediately. The basic preparation can be done in advance and the dish carefully re-heated before the eggs and cream are added.

Serves 4

1 lb smoked haddock fillets
Milk
8 oz long grain Patna rice
1½ oz butter
2 hard-boiled eggs
Salt and freshly ground black pepper
1 egg
¼ pint cream

Place the haddock fillets in a deep frying pan, cover with milk and simmer gently for about 10 minutes until the haddock will flake easily. Drain off the milk, remove any skin and bones and flake the fish with a fork.

Cook the rice in boiling salted water for about 20 minutes until tender. Drain well, rinse in cold water and drain well again. Roughly chop the hard-boiled eggs.

Melt the butter in a frying pan over a low heat. Add the rice and haddock and heat through. Gently mix in the hard-boiled eggs and season with salt and pepper. Combine the raw egg with cream and beat lightly. Pour the mixture over the kedgeree, mix lightly over the heat for about 1½ minutes until the mixture is creamy and serve at once.

Haddock Monte Carlo

This is a regular dish on the menus of some of the more established London restaurants and clubs, and a popular recipe of my parent's generation.

Serves 4

1½ lb smoked haddock fillets
4 large ripe tomatoes
1 oz butter

Salt and pepper
¼ pint milk
¼ pint single cream
6 eggs

Place the haddock fillets in a shallow saucepan and pour over the milk and cream. Simmer gently for about 15 minutes until the haddock is just tender. Drain off and reserve the cooking liquor and carefully skin the fish, removing any bones.

Drop the tomatoes into boiling water for 2 minutes and slide off the skins. Halve the tomatoes, remove the cores and seeds and chop the flesh. Poach the eggs in boiling water until just set, slide them on to a plate and trim the edges if necessary with kitchen scissors.

Arrange the tomatoes in a shallow serving dish. Cover the tomatoes with the cooked haddock fillets, arrange the eggs on top, and then pour over the cooking liquor, straining it through a fine sieve. Heat through in a hot oven (425° F. Reg. 7) for 5–10 minutes and serve at once.

HERRING

Marinated Baked Herrings or Mackerel

Plain food but nevertheless extremely tasty as a first course or a cold main course when served with a salad and a baked potato in its jacket.

Serves 4

4 herrings or medium-sized mackerel
1 large onion
¼ pint red wine vinegar
¼ pint water
1 tablespoon tomato ketchup
½ teaspoon dry English mustard
3 bay leaves
1 tablespoon finely chopped parsley
12 peppercorns
2 oz demerara sugar
½ teaspoon turmeric
Salt

Ask your fishmonger to clean and fillet the fish. Place the fillets, skin side down in a baking dish. Peel and thinly slice the onion, separate into rings and arrange over the fish. Combine the vinegar, water, tomato ketchup, mustard, peppercorns, parsley and bay leaves, mix well and season with a little salt. Pour the marinade over the fish, cover with foil and bake in a moderate oven (350° F. Reg. 4) for 1 hour. Remove the foil, sprinkle the combined turmeric and sugar over the fish and return to the oven for a further 15 minutes.

Leave the fish to cool in the liquid. Remove the peppercorns and bay leaves and pour off most of the excess liquid and serve cold with a garnish of fresh parsley.

Marinated or Soused Herrings

Herrings, rich in flavour and oil, must be eaten absolutely fresh. As straight from the sea to the oven as possible, this traditional way of cooking them is hard to beat. For some reason herrings have a kind of built-in snobbism about them, but if you pass them over as a first course for a dinner party you and your guests will be missing something with a sophisticated flavour at a very realistic price.

Serves 6 as a first course or 4 as a main course

> 4 herrings, washed, scaled and filleted,
> with heads and tails removed
> 2 shallots or small onions
> 1 medium-sized carrot
> 2 dried chillies
> 1 stick celery
> 2 bay leaves
> 8 peppercorns
> 1 tablespoon finely chopped parsley
> $\frac{1}{8}$ teaspoon salt
> $\frac{1}{2}$ pint white wine or cider vinegar
> $\frac{1}{2}$ pint water or very weak cold tea

Lay the fillets cut side up and, using a very sharp knife, cut off any rib bones. Cut down the centre of each fillet and trim off the back fin. Arrange the fillets, skin side down, in a shallow, fireproof dish.

Peel and very finely slice the shallots and divide into rings. Peel and very thinly slice the carrot. Remove the seeds of the chillies and chop the flesh. Clean the celery stalk, remove the leaves and thinly slice the stalk.

Arrange the shallots, carrots, chillies and celery slices over the fish and sprinkle over the parsley, peppercorns and salt. Top with the bay leaves. Combine the vinegar and water or weak tea and pour over the herrings. Cover tightly with tinfoil and bake in a warm oven (300° F. Reg. 2) for $1\frac{1}{4}$ hours. Leave to cool in the juices, refrigerate for 24 to 48 hours and then remove the herring fillets, roll them up neatly and garnish with some of the onion rings, carrot slices and celery.

As a first course, serve the herring fillets with thin slices of brown bread and butter.

As a main course, serve the herrings with lettuce, sliced, peeled cucumber and a potato salad.

Marinated Kippers with Hard-Boiled Eggs

Although this is by no means a traditional British recipe and does, in fact, have its origins in Scandinavia, I felt it was well worth including in this book because it makes such good use of one of our most delicious natural resources – the kipper. The hard-boiled eggs reduce the somewhat sharp flavour of this dish but they can be replaced by creamy scrambled eggs as a change.

Serves 6

> 4 kippers (2 pairs)
> 1 tablespoon finely chopped parsley
> $\frac{1}{2}$ tablespoon finely chopped fresh
> tarragon (or a pinch of dried tarragon)
> 1 tablespoon finely chopped chives
> 1 small onion
> 3 hard-boiled eggs
> 1 tablespoon white wine vinegar
> 3 tablespoons olive oil
> 1 teaspoon made English mustard
> Salt and freshly ground black pepper

Cut the heads and tails off the kippers and, using a sharp knife, remove the backbone, the skin and any other bones large enough to see. Cut the flesh of the kippers into ½-inch diagonal strips and arrange them in a serving dish. Peel and finely chop onion.

Mix the wine vinegar with the mustard and stir until smooth. Gradually blend in the olive oil. Mix in the parsley, tarragon and chives and season with salt and pepper. Pour the dressing over the kippers and chill in a refrigerator for 3 hours.

Peel the hard-boiled eggs and chop the whites. Rub the yolks through a fine sieve. Mix the egg whites with the kippers and onion and top with yolks. Serve well chilled with hot toast and butter.

Oatmealed Herrings with Mustard Sauce

I am not a great lover of herrings except in a marinated or pickled form, but I do like them if they are cooked in the following traditionally British way. Scoring the fish and rubbing them with mustard and a little lemon juice before coating them in oatmeal is an addition of my own; it gives the herrings extra flavour and helps to dispel that slightly fatty quality. Herrings, by the way, don't freeze well.

Serves 4

4 medium-sized herrings
1 teaspoon French Dijon mustard
2 teaspoons lemon juice
Oatmeal
Salt and pepper
1½ oz butter, melted

The sauce
1 small onion
1 oz butter
1 tablespoon flour
2 teaspoons French Dijon mustard
1½ gills milk
3 tablespoons single cream
Salt and pepper

Clean and scale the herrings and remove their heads and tails. Using a sharp knife cut diagonal scores along both sides of the fish, about six on each side, about ⅛ inch deep. Rub the mustard into the cuts and rub a little lemon juice over each fish. Coat the herrings in oatmeal, seasoned with salt and pepper.

Next make the sauce: peel and finely chop the onion. Melt 1 oz butter in a small saucepan, add the onion and cook over a medium low heat until the onion is soft and transparent. Mix in the flour and the mustard and gradually blend in the milk, stirring continually until the sauce comes to the boil and is smooth. Simmer for 5 minutes and then stir in the cream, season with salt and pepper and heat through without boiling.

Brush the herrings with the melted butter and grill under a high heat for about 4 minutes on each side until the skin is very crisp (almost burnt in places) and the fish are cooked through. Serve with the sauce on the side, with mashed potatoes and a green vegetable.

SALMON

Undoubtedly this is the king of all British fish. Surprisingly, it has also risen less in price than almost any other variety. In comparison to the more expensive cuts of meat it sells at a very realistic price at the height of its season, and last year, in the West Country, I was actually able to buy salmon more cheaply than at any time during the last fifteen years.

One of the most criminal of all culinary acts is to overcook this grand fish so that the flesh becomes dry and loses that silken, creamy texture that makes it so special. One Scotsman I know, who takes both the catching and eating of salmon most seriously, believes that the flesh should still be raw where it is attached to the backbone. I would not go that far but I would rather have his method any day than have the fish destroyed by overcooking. *Note:* Although salmon is still relatively expensive, salmon heads can be bought cheaply from some fishmongers. The gently poached head (poached in the same way as a whole fish) can provide a fair quantity of rich flesh for use in recipes like potted salmon, kedgeree and fish cakes.

Hard Roe from a Salmon

If you are able either to fish your own salmon or to buy it fresh from a fisherman, you may find a wealth of soft and hard roe in the stomach when you gut the fish. The soft roe is not particularly tasty but the hard roe is too good to overlook. It can be prepared in two ways:

1. This is a rather messy, cumbersome process but well worth the effort. Wash the red-grained caviar of a salmon under cold running water. Split the protective membrane with your fingernail and carefully scrape the caviar from the skin, picking it over carefully so that all membrane is removed. Rinse the caviar in very cold water, drain well and season with salt and pepper. Use the caviar as a garnish for soups or combined with cream cheese as a filling for savoury pancakes.

2. To make a salad of salmon caviar wash the roe under cold running water. Combine 2 pints of water with the juice of 1 lemon and ½ teaspoon salt and bring to the boil. Add the roe and poach for 8 minutes. Drain, plunge into cold water and drain again. Sandwich between two plates and leave until cold. Remove the outer membrane and cut the roe into small dice. Combine it with equal quantities of cold, diced potatoes, some thinly sliced celery sticks, chopped chives and mayonnaise. Mix lightly and serve on crisp lettuce leaves as a first or main course depending on the quantity.

Poached Salmon – to serve hot

This method varies from the cooking method used for salmon that is to be served cold. The salmon must be lifted straight from the water as soon as it is cooked and if absolutely necessary can be kept warm for a short time by being covered with a cloth that has been warmed in the oven.

> 1 salmon
> Water
> 4 tablespoons olive oil
> ½ lemon, cut into slices
> 4 oz salt to each gallon of water
> 1 onion, peeled and sliced
> 12 peppercorns

Scale and gut the fish, cleaning it well to ensure that no blood remains in the stomach.

Place the salmon in a fish kettle and rub it with the olive oil. Pour over just enough cold water to cover. Add the salt, onion, lemon and peppercorns.

Bring to the boil as quickly as possible, remove all the scum from the surface and then cover and simmer very gently, so that the water is only just moving, until the fish is just cooked. This will take about 1 hour for an 8-lb salmon but the only way to really tell is to pierce a small knife blade through the skin to the backbone in the fattest part of the fish. It will be ready when the flesh is just on the point of coming away from the bone.

Serve on a napkin, garnish with slices of lemon and sprigs of parsley and have with it cucumber slices in vinegar and plenty of melted butter.

Poached Salmon – to serve cold

Prepare the salmon exactly as above but bring it *slowly* to the boil and as soon as it is boiling remove the fish kettle from the stove and leave it in a cool place until cold. By this method any sized fish should be cooked through but not able to dry out. Some of the water can be replaced by a dry white wine to give an extra flavour to the flesh of the fish.

As soon as the fish is cold, lift out and drain well. Place on a large serving dish and carefully remove all the skin. Mask with home-made mayonnaise and garnish with slices of cucumber and lemon.

Potted Salmon

Leftover salmon, if there ever is such a thing, makes an excellent kedgeree or very superior fishcakes. It can also be potted to use as a first course or in sandwiches.

Serves 4

½ lb salmon
4 oz butter, melted
Salt and freshly ground black pepper
Pinch mace

Remove any skin or bone from the salmon and flake the flesh. Gradually add the melted butter, beating with a wooden spoon until the mixture is nearly smooth. Season with salt and pepper, add a little mace and pack in an earthenware dish. Chill in a refrigerator until firm.

If you wish to keep the salmon for some days, cover it with a film of clarified butter.

SEAFOOD AND OTHER FISH

Cockles

In many places along the coast of Britain it is still possible to buy cockles that have not been soused in vinegar; in Looe on the south coast of Cornwall one can even buy them still in their shells and make a delicious dish like *Moules Marinières* from them. Fresh cockles, in a white sauce with onions and cheese, make an inexpensive first course.

Serves 4

8 oz cockles
1 onion
½ oz butter
2 tablespoons flour
½ pint milk
1 tablespoon finely chopped parsley
White pepper
2 oz grated cheese
2 tablespoons fine browned breadcrumbs

Peel and very finely chop the onion. Melt the butter in a saucepan, add the onion and cook over a medium low heat until the onion is soft and transparent. Add the flour and mix well. Gradually add the milk, stirring continually until the sauce comes to the boil and is thick and smooth. Add the parsley, season with pepper and simmer for 4 minutes. Mix in the cockles and turn into 4 scallop shells or ramekin dishes. Combine the cheese and breadcrumbs, sprinkle them over the cockle mixture and brown under a hot grill.

Grilled Lobsters

Nowhere are the lobsters better than those caught around our shores; sweet, tender and succulent – why else would they be sent across by plane to France daily?

Pickled walnuts, like anchovies, used to be in general use as a flavouring ingredient and their sparing use in this delicious hot shellfish dish brings out the flavour of the lobster.

Serves 4

2 small-boiled lobsters (¾–1 lb each)

2 shallots

2 oz butter

1 tablespoon flour

½ pint milk

¼ pint double cream

2 egg yolks

2 teaspoons freshly chopped tarragon

(or ¼ teaspoon dried tarragon)

2 tablespoons brandy

¼ teaspoon paprika

2 pickled walnuts, finely chopped

Salt and pepper

1½ oz grated cheese

2 tablespoons finely grated stale white breadcrumbs

Remove the claws and legs of the lobsters. Spread the lobsters on a wooden board and, using a large, sharp pointed knife, cut them straight down the centre of the back of the shell from the head to the end of the tail.

Separate the lobsters into halves and remove and discard the stomach sacs from the head (small transparent sacs usually containing gritty, discoloured matter) and ease out and discard the thin, black intestine line running through the flesh of the tail.

Take out all the flesh from the body and tail. Crack the claws and the legs and remove all the meat from the shells. Cut the flesh into thin slices.

Beat the egg yolks with the cream. Peel and finely slice shallots. Melt 1½ oz butter in a saucepan, add the shallots and cook gently over a low heat until shallots are soft and transparent. Add the flour, mix well and gradually blend in the milk, stirring continually until the sauce is thick and smooth. Add the tarragon. Blend in the cream and egg yolks, mix in the brandy, paprika, walnuts and lobster and season with salt and pepper.

Fill the shells with the lobster mixture. Cover with breadcrumbs, sprinkle over the cheese and dribble over the remaining butter, melted. Place the filled shells in a fireproof dish and grill under a moderately high heat until the lobsters are hot through and the top is a golden brown. Serve at once.

Devilled Prawn Savoury

Serves 4

4 oz peeled prawns
½ oz butter
1 tablespoon tomato chutney
Few drops Worcestershire sauce and Tabasco
Salt and pepper
Small pinch of cayenne
1 tablespoon flour
½ oz butter
¼ pint milk (preferably gold top)
1½ oz finely grated Cheddar cheese
½ teaspoon made English mustard
4 slices bread
Lard for frying

Melt ½ oz butter in a small pan. Add the prawns, tomato chutney, Worcester and Tabasco sauce and season with a little salt, pepper and cayenne and cook over a medium high heat until hot through. Keep warm.

Melt ½ oz butter in a clean saucepan, add the flour and mix well. Gradually add the milk, stirring continually over a medium heat until the sauce is thick and smooth. Mix in the cheese and mustard, season with salt and pepper and cook gently until the cheese is melted.

Remove the crusts from the bread, cut each slice in half and fry the pieces of bread in hot lard until they are golden brown on both sides. Drain the fried bread on kitchen paper and arrange slices in a shallow baking dish. Cover the bread with prawns and top with the cheese sauce. Brown under a hot grill until the cheese is bubbling and golden on top. Serve at once. For a supper or luncheon dish, serve with a watercress salad and grilled tomatoes.

Devilled Whitebait

I could eat whitebait every day of my life if I could get them. Once I did and although I was then very small I still remember the event with longing. It was during the war and we had been evacuated to a seaside resort called Tenby in Wales. One afternoon shoals and shoals of tiny fish swam into the harbour; everyone rushed down with buckets and we stood up to our knees in the water just scooping them out by the hundred. I remember other people saying they ate so much whitebait then they never wanted to see the things again, but that certainly wasn't the case with me.

If you have to use frozen whitebait, let them thaw out in the refrigerator, drain them well and then pat dry carefully on a cloth or kitchen paper. Damp fish will not fry to the delicious crispness that makes these so special.

Serves 4

1 lb whitebait
¼ teaspoon dry English mustard
¼ teaspoon cayenne pepper
Salt
Flour
Deep oil for frying
Thin slices of brown buttered bread
Quarters of lemon

Combine enough flour to give the whitebait a good coating with the mustard and cayenne, season with salt and mix well. Place the seasoned flour in a large bag, add the whitebait and shake until the fish are coated all over.

Heat the oil until smoking, add the fish, not too many at a time, and cook for 3 minutes. Drain on kitchen paper. Reheat the oil between each batch and when they are all cooked, return them altogether to the hot oil for 1 minute only. Drain again and serve at once with the brown bread and lemon quarters. *Note:* If you should happen to have any whitebait left over, dress them with a little vinaigrette dressing and serve them cold as a first course.

Baked Mackerel with Cider

Serves 4

4 large mackerel
1 large onion
1 lemon
1 apple
½ pint dry cider
1 tablespoon vinegar
Salt and 8 peppercorns
4 bay leaves
1 tablespoon finely chopped parsley

Clean the mackerel and cut off the head and tails, and cut out the backbones to make fillets (your fishmonger will do this for you). Peel the onion, cut into thin slices and separate into rings. Peel, core and thinly slice the apples. Crush the peppercorns.

Arrange the onions in a lightly greased baking dish. Place the mackerel fillets on top and cover with the apple slices. Add the peppercorns, season with salt and place the bay leaves on top. Pour over the cider and vinegar, cover tightly with foil and bake in a moderate oven (350° F. Reg. 4) for 40 minutes. Remove the foil and bay leaves and leave to cool. Serve chilled, sprinkled with the chopped parsley. *Note:* The mackerel can be served hot in which case a white sauce should be made by melting ½ oz butter, adding 1 tablespoon flour and then mixing in the strained juices from the dish. Pour the sauce over the mackerel, onion and apple, heat through in a moderate oven and sprinkle with the parsley before serving with lemon wedges.

Mock Crab

Although this dish takes time to prepare it makes a delicious summer salad, especially for outdoor eating.

Serves 4

½ lb halibut or hake fillet
4 oz Cheddar cheese
½ gill white wine vinegar
½ teaspoon dry mustard

1 teaspoon anchovy essence

White pepper and a pinch cayenne

1 crisp lettuce

1 teaspoon finely chopped shallot

or two spring onions

1 small cucumber

1½ gills mayonnaise

Steam the fish in a lightly greased colander over boiling water for about 10 minutes until just tender. Leave to cool and then divide carefully into large flakes.

Finely grate the cheese, combine it in a basin with the vinegar, mustard, anchovy essence, pepper and cayenne and mash with a fork until the mixture is smooth. Using a small spoon spread a little of the mixture on each fish flake.

Clean the lettuce and shred it finely. Peel a cucumber and cut it into very small dice. Arrange the lettuce, the diced cucumber and the shallot or spring onion in a salad bowl. Top with the flakes of fish and spoon over the mayonnaise. Chill before serving. This dish can also be served as a first course.

3
Meat

Fashions in meat buying and cooking have changed and with them our eating habits. Some of these habits seem to be coming full circle and it is interesting, for instance, that there is a tendency these days to return to the Elizabethan practice of spicing and seasoning our meat. This was a necessity for the Elizabethans, to preserve the meat and possibly to overcome a high or rancid taste which was the result of inadequate storage facilities. In our case it is due more to the tastelessness of meat in the present day. Breeders and butchers are in such a hurry to get meat from the fields to the housewife that it is inadequately hung and much of the flavour is lost. Mutton has almost completely disappeared and the rather insipid imported lamb is frequently easier to buy than our own mountain or valley breeds. Pork, which used to be well covered in fat (essential for smoking and curing processes), is now bred to be so lean that I often find it actually tough.

Other meat-eating habits are also reversing. As Britain became prosperous offal and the cheaper cuts of meat became the lot of the poor, something to turn one's nose up at. Now that all kinds of meat have risen horrifically in price it has become necessary for many of us to search round for these cheaper cuts once more and, although it is no longer easy to find pig's ears or trotters, the practice of slow-cooking such things as shin beef and ox heart is having a definite revival.

British beef is still among the finest in the world and I find it heartbreaking that the hanging process is so seldom carried out these days. Well hung beef is still served in some of the best of our restaurants and can be found in those few butchers' shops which deal only in the highest quality and who charge high prices for their meat; most of us, sadly, have to make do with second best and a flavour our grandparents would have frowned upon. Frustration in this direction has led me to 'hanging' my own beef, buying joints that I know have not been frozen, covering any cut areas with plastic film to prevent the blood seeping out and keeping them in the bottom of the refrigerator for about five days before cooking. This process in no way duplicates the standard of an animal that is hung whole but it is certainly an improvement.

Although pork is never hung there is still the problem of lack

of fat with the present-day lean animals. Try to buy pork joints
that have a good layer of fat around them and if you happen to
dislike the extra richness that fat gives the meat, counteract it by
the use of those herbs and spices which go well with pork.

Mutton was once our pride but lamb was more frequently eaten
in the Mediterranean countries, from which we have learned to
cook our lamb with rosemary and lemon. Traditional roasts of
saddle of lamb and guard of honour, however, still remain classic
British dishes and can be truly delicious if they are made of young
English lamb and not from imported meat. New Zealand lamb,
which is often tender but frequently lacking in flavour, can be improved by marinading and again by the subtle use of herbs and spices.

Commercially made meat pies have ruined the reputation of
much of our traditional British fare and although you can find
some delicious, mouth-watering pork pies in the Midlands and the
north of England, they are few and far between. Try making your
own; the effort is infinitely rewarding and the pies can, of course,
be stored in a deep freeze.

Try making your own sausages too. By doing so you will dis-
cover what is in them and not be left wondering what on earth
many of the commercial varieties contain that makes them taste
of plastic. Old-fashioned herb sausages, the traditional coiled, un-
linked sausage from Cumberland and your own variations of
seasoning can produce meals that will fill the kitchen with
fabulous aromas. Fortunately it is still possible to buy good black
and West Country hog's pudding (more complicated for the
housewife to produce) and these two make inexpensive eating and
are good to eat fried in slices and served with fried apple slices
and onion rings. If you make your own sausage mixture a good
butcher can pack it in skins for you, and although your home-
made products will obviously not contain preservatives they will
keep for up to 2 months in a deep freeze.

In the realm of meat cookery things may not be what they
were, but at least we can still produce a steak and kidney pudding
that restores one's faith in British cooking – especially if it has
added to it that cunning leavening of oysters, no longer a penny
a bushel but still so very, very good.

To Make Good Gravy

The secret of a good, well-flavoured gravy is in the making, and provides the finishing touch to a roast joint or bird. Don't take the lazy way out by brewing up a synthetic mixture of powdered gravy mix or stock cubes thickened with flour; a little extra time and trouble, using natural, wholesome ingredients will complement and enrich any main dish you serve.

Gravy for Roast Meat

Remove the meat from the roasting pan 5 minutes before you plan to serve it and leave it to settle on a serving dish in a warm place (this makes the meat more compact and leads to more economical carving). Drain off all but about 3 tablespoons from the juices in the pan, straining them through a fine sieve. Return all the residue from the sieve to the roasting tin and place over a low heat. Add 2 tablespoons plain flour, mix well with a wooden spoon and continue to stir until the flour is well browned. Gradually add 1–1½ pints of stock or water that has been well flavoured from having vegetables cooked in it. Bring the gravy to the boil, stirring all the time, and cook for 4 minutes. Strain into a gravy dish and spoon off any fat that rises to the surface just before serving.

Using Leftover Gravy

Keep leftover gravy in a covered jar or pot in the refrigerator for up to 4 days and use it to give strength and flavour to soups, sauces and stews.

Using Leftover Juices from Roast Meat

On any occasion when a sauce rather than a gravy is required to accompany roast meat or poultry, do not throw away the juices left in the pan. These constitute the old-fashioned 'meat glaze' and can be invaluable to add taste, goodness and flavour to a great number of dishes, especially soups, sauces and stews.

Drain off excess fat and pour the meat juices into a jar or pot, scraping in every residue in the pan. Cool and refrigerate, skimming off the fat when it has set. The meat glaze can be kept for at least a week.

BEEF

Abovetown Underroast

A good combination of shin beef and kidney with a crisp topping of potatoes.

Serves 4–6

2 lb shin beef
8 oz kidney
Flour
2 tablespoons dripping
1 lb onions
2 large carrots
8 oz swede
Salt and freshly ground black pepper
1¼ pints stock
1½ lb potatoes

Remove any tough sinews from the meat and cut it into small dice. Trim the hard centre core from the kidney and cut into small pieces. Peel and roughly chop the onions. Peel and dice the carrots and swede. Peel the potatoes and cut into pieces about the size of a small egg.

Combine some flour with a generous seasoning of salt and pepper. Roll the meat in seasoned flour until well coated. Melt the dripping in a flameproof casserole, add the meat and brown over a high heat on all sides. Remove the meat with a slotted spoon. Add the onions, carrots and swede to the juices in the casserole and cook over a lowish heat until the onions are soft and transparent. Add the meat, pour over the stock, bring to the boil, cover and simmer for 30 minutes.

Place the potatoes on top of the stew so that they are half in and half out of the stock. Do not replace the cover of the casserole. Cook in a moderate oven (325° F. Reg. 3) for 2 hours until the meat is cooked and the tops of the potatoes are crisp and golden brown.

Boiled Beef and Dumplings

With this recipe there is plenty of meat leftover for *rechauffé* dishes.

Serves 6

4 lb brisket or silverside
2 tablespoons salt
Plenty of freshly ground black pepper
Bouquet garni
12 small onions or shallots
4 large carrots
1 small turnip
2 large leeks

Dumplings
4 oz self-raising flour
Salt and pepper
¼ teaspoon sage
½ teaspoon thyme
2 oz shredded suet
Water to mix

Place the meat in a large, heavy saucepan, add the salt, pepper and bouquet garni, cover with cold water and bring slowly to the boil. Skim off any scum from the surface, cover and simmer very slowly for 2½ hours. Peel the onions. Peel and roughly chop the carrots and turnip. Clean and slice the leeks. Add the vegetables to the meat, bring back to the boil and simmer for a further 30 minutes.

To make the dumplings combine the flour, herbs and suet, season with salt and pepper and add enough cold water to make a firm dough. Flour your hands and divide the dough into twelve pieces and form into balls. Add the dumplings to the meat and continue to simmer for a further 20 minutes or until all the dumplings have risen to the surface of the pan.

Remove the meat from the saucepan and place it in the centre of a large, heated serving dish. Lift out the vegetables and dumplings from the stock with a slotted spoon and arrange them around the meat. Serve some of the stock separately and keep the rest to make an excellent soup base.

Braised Flank of Beef with Celery

Flank is a cheap cut of beef which can be used to make a very satisfactory dish. Any leftover makes good mince for leftover dishes and any remaining celery can be added to soup.

Serves 6

3 lb flank of beef, boned and rolled
1½ heads of celery
¼ pint stock
Salt and freshly ground black pepper
Pinch of allspice

Remove the leaves of the celery and any tough strings from the side of the sticks and cut into 2-inch lengths. Place the meat in a heavy casserole and surround with the celery. Season with salt, pepper and allspice, pour over the stock and cover very tightly. Cook in a moderate oven (350° F. Reg. 4) for 3 hours or until the meat is tender.

Callops with Poached Eggs

Adding oatmeal instead of fresh breadcrumbs to minced beef makes it go further and adds an interesting flavour to the meat. Although this dish originated in Scotland, variations of it appear in many parts of the country.

Serves 4

1 lb good minced beef
1 large onion
1 tablespoon oatmeal
½ pint stock
1½ tablespoons finely chopped parsley
Salt and freshly ground black pepper
1 oz butter or dripping
1½ lbs mashed potatoes
4 eggs

Peel and very finely chop the onion. Melt the butter or dripping in a heavy pan. Add the onion and beef and cook over a high heat, stirring frequently, until the meat is well browned. Add the oatmeal, stock and 1 tablespoon parsley, season with salt and pepper. Cover and simmer for 30 minutes or until the meat is really tender.

Arrange a ring of mashed potatoes around a serving dish and put the callops in the centre. Poach the eggs, arrange them on the meat, sprinkle over remaining parsley and serve at once.

A Cornish Pasty – the real thing

You cannot live in Cornwall for fifteen years without learning a good deal about a pasty. By trial and error, I also discovered that it takes an expert to make the real thing and it was Julie, Cornish born and bred, who eventually taught me the tricks of the trade. 'A real pasty,' she said, 'wasn't just meat and vegetables sandwiched up in a circle of pastry; it was a full meal with the meat one end and the pudding at the other, a meal that would satisfy a man – the sort of man who had to do a full day's work.' The following recipe is a facsimile of the recipe for the pasties taken to work by tin miners in the nineteenth century when Cornwall was in its zenith and men had real hearty appetites.

Julie still makes my pasties, and long may she go on doing so. If I want the ideal picnic food for point-to-points, shooting parties or long sorties to the beach, these man-sized pasties are the food I choose every time.

I make no apologies for the detailed length of this recipe. It sounds complicated, but once you have the knack, I promise you will not regret any early frustrations.

Serves 5

2 lb self-raising flour
¾ lb margarine
3 gills water

Filling
1 lb potatoes
2 small onions
1 lb beef skirt (fat removed)
1 small turnip
Salt and pepper
1½ oz butter
1 small beaten egg
4 oz sugar
2 lb cooking apples

To make the pastry sieve the flour into a large basin. Add the margarine, cut into small pieces and then cut the margarine into the flour using two sharp knives, and continue to cut until the mixture resembles coarse breadcrumbs. Add the water, mix by hand until the mixture forms a firm dough, place in a polythene bag and chill for at least 20 minutes.

To prepare the filling cut the beef into thin slivers using a sharp knife (some people mince their meat for pasties but this really does ruin the flavour). Peel and finely chop the onion. Peel and coarsely grate the turnip and the potato. Cover the potatoes and turnip with cold water until required.

Peel, core and thickly slice the apples and cover them with cold water until required.

Using a well-floured board roll out the pastry to $\frac{1}{8}$ inch thickness large enough to cut into five circles using a 10-inch dinner plate as a guide. From the remaining dough, rolled out thinly, cut five triangles, roughly $3\frac{1}{4}$ inches on each side for the dividing layer. Dip one edge of a dividing triangle in water and press it firmly across the centre of a pastry circle. Repeat with remaining circles.

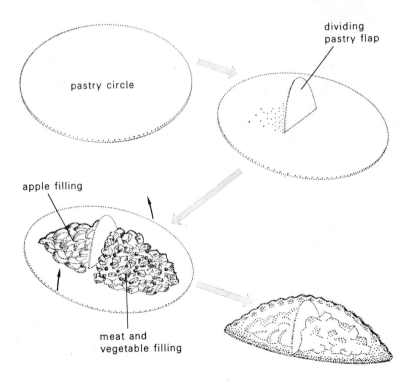

pastry circle

dividing pastry flap

apple filling

meat and vegetable filling

Place the meat, potato, turnip and onion on one side of the dividing layer and the apples on the other side (drain all the ingredients before placing on pastry). Season the savoury side of the pasties with salt and pepper mixed with a small knob of softened butter and flavour the apple side with sugar. Bring the edges of the pastry together so that the dividing layer triangle forms a barrier through the centre, moisten all the edges well (no juice should be allowed to seep through from the savoury to the sweet side) and crimp the top edges of the pasty together to make a neat ridge. Make a small cross or other symbol on one end of the pasty to indicate the savory end. Brush the pasties with beaten egg and bake in a hot oven (400° F. Reg. 6) for 20 minutes and then reduce the heat to moderate (325° F. Reg. 3) for a further 5–10 minutes until the meat is tender (make a small slit and test the filling). See diagram.

Leave to cool for 15 minutes before eating from your hands from the savoury end towards the pudding course.

If the pasties are to be taken on a picnic, wrap them in generous layers of newspaper and pack them tightly in a cardboard box; they will retain some of their heat for a considerable length of time.

Mushroom Pocket Steaks

Once the traveller, making his way through England and stopping for sustenance at a wayside inn, would have been offered as a snack a tender carpet bag steak of rare fillet stuffed with succulent oysters. Gone are the days when oysters were a penny a bushel and to be able to open and beard them by the dozen was an integral part of a housewife's art. Now, one usually has to make do with the choice of overcooked chicken, curiously served in a basket, or monk fish masquerading as scampi.

Firm mushrooms, thinly sliced and lightly cooked, have a remarkable similarity to the texture of oysters. This dish may not have the richness of the true carpet bag steak, but it does have a delicacy of its own that is very memorable.

Serves 4

4 fillet steaks, ¾ inch thick
4 oz firm button mushrooms
2½ oz butter
1 tablespoon flour

1 teaspoon made English mustard
1 tablespoon finely chopped parsley
3 tablespoons double cream
$\frac{1}{4}$ teaspoon Worcestershire sauce
$\frac{1}{4}$ tablespoon brandy
Salt and freshly ground black pepper
1 egg beaten,
Dried breadcrumbs
Sprigs of parsley
2 tablespoons olive oil

Lightly beat the steaks and remove all fat and gristle. Cut a pocket into the sides of the steaks, using a sharp knife, and gently cut until the slit is as large as possible without breaking through the outer edges.

Slice the mushrooms very thinly. Melt 1 oz butter, add the mushrooms and cook over a low heat for 1 minute. Stir in the flour and blend in the cream, stirring lightly until the sauce is smooth but taking care not to let the mixture boil. Add the chopped parsley, brandy and Worcestershire sauce, season with salt and pepper and leave the mixture to cool. Stuff the filling into the steaks, rub the outer surfaces with a little mustard and dip each one in beaten egg and breadcrumbs. Season with salt and pepper.

Heat the oil and $1\frac{1}{2}$ oz butter together in a frying pan until butter foams, add the steaks and cook over a high heat for about $2\frac{1}{2}$ minutes on each side until the coating is crisp and golden brown.

Remove steaks and drain them on kitchen paper. Place on a hot serving dish and surround with sprigs of parsley quickly fried until crisp and also drained on kitchen paper. Serve with potatoes and a green vegetable or green salad.

Rich Oxtail Stew

Serves 6

2 oxtails
1 tablespoon dripping
3 tablespoons flour
Salt and freshly ground black pepper
18 small shallots

4 large carrots
3 pints beef stock
4 tablespoons tomato purée
2 oz sultanas
Juice and grated rind of 1 lemon
Bouquet garni and 3 bay leaves
2 tablespoons finely chopped parsley

Ask your butcher to divide the tails into joints when you buy them. Cover the tails with cold water and leave to soak for 4 hours or overnight. Drain and wipe dry. Roll the oxtail joints in well-seasoned flour.

Melt the dripping in a large heavy pan, add the tail and cook over a high heat until the joints are browned on all sides. Add the stock (the joints should be covered; add a little cold water if necessary), season with salt and pepper and add the bouquet garni and bay leaves. Bring to the boil, skim off any scum which rises to the surface, cover and simmer for 2 hours. Discard the bay leaves and bouquet garni, remove the meat from the stock and leave the stock to cool and then chill in a refrigerator until any fat forms a solid skin on the surface. Remove the fat. Peel the shallots and blanch them in boiling water for 5 minutes. Peel and dice the carrots. Return the oxtail joints to the stock, add the shallots, carrots, sultanas, lemon juice and rind, bring to the boil, stir in the tomato purée, cover and simmer for a further 1–1½ hours until the meat is just beginning to fall from the bones. Sprinkle with the chopped parsley before serving.

Roast Beef of Old England

Everyone, you might say, knows how to roast a joint of beef. This recipe will, I hope, tell you how to give it just a little bit more flavour and succulence.

Serves 6–8

5 lb sirloin with fillet, on the bone
2 tablespoons dripping or suet,
or some fat bacon rinds
1 clove garlic
1 shallot
1 teaspoon brown sugar

½ tablespoon flour
2 tablespoons red wine
¼ pint beef stock
Salt and freshly ground black pepper

Rub the joint with plenty of freshly ground black pepper and the peeled garlic clove and leave to stand for 2 hours. Rub the meat with the dripping or place the suet or bacon rinds on top of it.

Place the meat on a rack in a roasting tin and cook in a hot oven (425° F. Reg. 7) for 15 minutes to the pound (add an extra 15 minutes for those who like their meat well cooked).

Place the meat on a serving dish and leave it to settle for 5 minutes – this makes the meat more compact and carving easier and more economical.

Drain off the fat from the pan (this can be done earlier during the cooking process to be used for making Yorkshire pudding), leaving about 1 tablespoon fat with the sediment in the tin. Add the shallot, peeled and finely chopped, and cook over a medium heat until the shallot is soft and transparent. Add the flour, mixing well to incorporate all the sediment, and blend in the stock, wine and sugar. Season with salt and pepper, stirring continually over a high heat until the gravy comes to the boil and is thickened and smooth. Strain the gravy into a gravy boat through a fine sieve.

Steamed Puddings with Suet Crusts

Steak and kidney are not the only ingredients that can form the fillings of succulent, nourishing boiled puddings and variations of savoury puddings used to be standard British fare, providing economical but satisfying main courses.

Suet pastry is simple and quick to make, cheaper cuts of meat can be used as the cooking process is lengthy and any extra cooking costs are offset by the inexpensive cost of the ingredients. This type of pastry also seals the ingredients in such a way that all the flavour and aroma of the contents are captured.

Unlike most other pastries, a suet crust is at its best and lightest if it is used as quickly as possible and not left to dry out. Use half quantities of shredded beef suet to self-raising flour, add just enough water to form a stiff dough, knead it only enough to make it smooth and reasonably pliable and roll out on a well floured board. When lining a pudding basin with suet crust, don't worry about any pleats or cracks in the pastry; these can be smoothed out with your fingers.

Cover the finished pudding with a double layer of greaseproof paper, a layer of tinfoil or a well floured cloth. Tie down the sides firmly with string and make a loop over the top so that the basin can be easily lifted out of the saucepan.

Measure the water to be used for steaming before starting your preparations (it should come three-quarters of the way up the basin) and put the prepared pudding straight into boiling water. Add more water during the cooking process, if necessary, and keep the pudding in steadily, gently boiling water.

Steak and Kidney Pudding – with or without Oysters

There are two schools of thought about the cooking of this delicious dish; those who say the filling should be put raw into the pastry crust and those who say it should be half cooked before being encased. I belong to the latter school for two reasons: (1) made with uncooked meat the pudding needs an extremely long steaming time and there is always the danger of the filling being slightly underdone at the end; (2) because cooking the meat filling on a ring is less expensive on fuel than cooking it in the oven and you need have no fear of the filling being tough.

If you cannot afford oysters, add some thickly sliced mushrooms and a touch of anchovy essence instead, and do add a little Worcester sauce and some bay leaves to the filling.

Serves 6

> 2 lb rump steak
> 1 lb ox kidney
> Flour
> Salt and pepper
> 2 onions
> 3 oz dripping or butter
> ½ pint good beef stock
> ½ pint red wine
> Pinch mixed herbs
> Pinch allspice

12 oysters (or 9 oz firm button mushrooms and
1 teaspoon anchovy essence)
3 bay leaves
Worcestershire sauce

Suet Crust

10 oz self-raising flour
1 teaspoon baking powder
Pinch mixed herbs
Salt and pepper
4 oz shredded suet
Water to mix

Cut the steak into 1-inch cubes. Remove any hard core from the kidney and cut into ½-inch pieces. Peel and chop the onion (thickly slice mushrooms if these are to be used). Roll the meat and kidney in well-seasoned flour.

Melt the dripping or butter in a flameproof casserole, add the onion and cook over a medium heat until golden. Remove the onion with a slotted spoon, add the meat and kidney to the juices in the dish and cook over a high heat, stirring continually, until browned on all sides. Add the stock and wine, mixing well to incorporate all the bits which have stuck to the bottom of the pan, add the onions and bring to the boil. Mix in the herbs, add about a half teaspoon of Worcestershire sauce and cook for 5 minutes.

Cover very tightly (if your lid doesn't fit properly put a layer of foil over the top of the dish before putting on the lid) and cook in a slow oven (300° F. Reg. 2) for 1½ hours. Check the seasoning of the gravy, remove the bay leaves, and leave to cool.

Make the suet crust by combining the flour, baking powder, salt and pepper, herbs and suet in a bowl and mixing well. Add just enough cold water to make a firm dough, kneading just enough to make the pastry smooth. Set aside a quarter of the pastry and roll out the rest on a well-floured board to make a large circle about ¼ inch thick.

Butter a 3-pint pudding basin and line it with the pastry, smoothing it against the sides with your hands and pressing out any creases – until the pastry is even. Add the oysters and their liquor (or the mushrooms and anchovy essence) to the filling and spoon it into the pastry case. Roll out the rest of the pastry to make a lid, pinching the edges together firmly. Butter a piece of greaseproof paper large enough to cover the bowl and overlap the sides and tie it over the edge of the bowl with string making a handle from one side to the other with extra string.

Place the bowl in a large saucepan and add enough water to the pan to come two-thirds of the way up the basin. Remove the basin, bring the water to the boil and then lower in the basin using the string handle. Cover with a lid and boil for 2 hours removing the lid for the last 20 minutes to firm the crust.

Check now and then to see that the water is not boiling away – if it does pour in more boiling water from a kettle.

Remove the greaseproof paper and wrap a white damask napkin around the bowl to serve.

Thursday Stew

Serves 4

1½ lb shin beef
Flour
Salt and freshly ground black pepper
4 oz streaky bacon
1½ tablespoons dripping
2 large onions
2 large carrots
Pinch ground cloves
Grated rind of 1 lemon
1 bay leaf
Pinch thyme
¼ lb firm button mushrooms
¾ pint strong beef stock

Cut the beef into 1-inch pieces. Remove the rinds of the bacon and chop the rashers. Peel and quarter the onions. Peel and chop the carrots.

Combine some flour with a generous seasoning of salt and pepper. Coat the meat in seasoned flour. Melt the dripping in a heavy flameproof casserole, add the bacon and meat and cook over a high heat, stirring every now and then until the meat is nicely browned on all sides. Add the vegetables, mushrooms and herbs and pour over the stock. Mix well, bring to the boil, cover and cook in a slow oven (300° F. Reg. 2) for about 3 hours or until the meat is tender.

Tickler's Pie

This is my interpretation of a recipe I was told about by an old codger who used to make most of his money by tickling the salmon from other people's rivers. His granny, he said, used to make a *real* Shepherd's Pie with the remains of the Sunday joint – a pie that had a bit of a bite to it. *Note:* Tickling, by the way, is the art of catching salmon and trout in the hands by tickling them or stroking them into a comatose state.

4 generous servings

1 lb cooked beef
2 onions
1 heaped tablespoon meat dripping
1 tablespoon flour
½ tablespoon curry powder
2 tablespoons tomato chutney
1 pint stock
1½ lb potatoes
½ oz butter
½ teaspoon made English mustard
2 oz grated Cheddar cheese
Salt and pepper

Coarsely mince the beef. Peel and very thinly slice the onions. Peel the potatoes and boil them until tender. Drain well and mash with the butter, mustard and half the cheese. Season the mashed potatoes with salt and pepper.

Melt the dripping in a large frying pan and add the onions. Cook over a low heat until the onions are soft and transparent. Add the meat, sprinkle over the flour and curry powder and mix well. Cook, stirring continually for 2 minutes and then gradually mix in the stock. Bring to the boil, cover and simmer for 20 minutes. Add the chutney, season with salt and pepper if necessary, and cook for a further 20 minutes.

Transfer the meat to a baking dish, spoon off any excess stock and spread the potatoes on top of the meat. Sprinkle over the

remaining cheese and bake in a hot oven (425° F. Reg. 7) for
10–15 minutes until the top is a delicious golden brown.

Union Beef Stew with Dumplings

Serves 4

1¼ *lb stewing steak (i.e. chuck)*
1 large onion
2 oz dripping
2 tablespoons flour
2 teaspoons made English mustard
2 teaspoons made horseradish sauce
1 pint beef stock
1 pint brown ale
1 teaspoon sugar
Salt and freshly ground black pepper
4 oz self-raising flour
2 oz shredded suet
1½ teaspoons mixed herbs
Water to mix

Cut the meat into 1½-inch cubes. Peel and chop the onion. Heat
the dripping in a heavy saucepan, add the onion and cook over a
medium heat until the onion is transparent. Remove the onion with
a slotted spoon. Add the meat to the dripping and cook over a high
heat, stirring frequently until the meat is well browned on all
sides. Sprinkle with the flour and mix well. Add the mustard and
horseradish sauce and gradually blend in the stock, beer and sugar.
Season with salt and pepper, and transfer to a heavy casserole.
Cover tightly and cook in a moderate oven (325° F. Reg. 3) for
1½ hours or until the meat is tender.

To make the dumplings: sieve the self-raising flour into a bowl
with a generous pinch of salt. Mix in the suet and herbs and make
a well in the centre. Stir in enough water to make a pliable dough.
Divide the mixture into eight and using floured hands roll into
eight balls.

Add the dumplings to the stew and continue to cook for a further
12–20 minutes.

LAMB

Crisped Breast of Lamb

Breast of lamb has always been one of the cheaper cuts of meat, but has the disadvantage of being fatty. In this recipe the fattiness is controlled and the result is an inexpensive dish I am extremely fond of. Serve it with a tomato sauce (see page 161).

Serves 4

2 lb breast of lamb
2 sprigs parsley
sprig thyme
2 bay leaves
1 onion
2 large carrots
Salt
8 peppercorns, crushed
1 egg, beaten
2 oz breadcrumbs
1 oz butter

Peel and roughly chop the onion and carrots. Place the meat in a heavy saucepan with the herbs, vegetables, salt and peppercorns and cover with boiling water. Return to the boil and simmer for about $1\frac{1}{2}$ hours or until the bones will slip easily from the meat. Remove the meat (the cooking liquid can be used as a stock base), leave to cool a little and then pull out the bones. Place the meat on a flat plate, cover with a second plate and weigh down with a heavy weight. Leave in a refrigerator for at least four hours.

Cut the meat into finger-size pieces, dip the pieces into beaten egg and then coat in breadcrumbs seasoned with a little salt and pepper. Fry the pieces in the butter until nicely crisp and golden brown and drain on kitchen paper. Serve with a spicy tomato sauce.

Chump Chops with Mint and Lemon Sauce

Serves 4

4 chump chops
Flour
Salt and pepper
1 oz butter
1 tablespoon olive oil
Rind and juice of 1 lemon
1½ tablespoons chopped mint
6 tablespoons water
2 tablespoons redcurrant jelly
1 bunch watercress

Dip the chops into seasoned flour until they are well coated. Melt the butter with the oil in a frying pan until really hot. Add the chops and cook over a low heat for about 7 minutes on each side. Drain the chops on kitchen paper, arrange on a serving dish and keep warm. Reserve 1½ tablespoons of the juices in the pan.

Combine the pan juices with the lemon rind, lemon peel, mint, water and redcurrant jelly. Cook over a low heat, stirring continually until the jelly has melted. Raise heat, bring to the boil and cook for a further 2 minutes.

Pour the sauce over the chops, garnish with the watercress and serve at once.

Eighteenth-century Hot Pot

A hot pot is always better if made the day before it is required and left to settle overnight so that any excess fat can be given time to rise to the surface of the stew. It can then be removed.

Serves 4

1½ lb lamb chops from the end of neck
2 lamb's kidneys
1 lb onions
1½ lb potatoes
Salt and freshly ground black pepper
Water
½ oz butter, melted

Cut the meat into chops. Peel and slice the onions and divide them into rings. Peel and thinly slice the potatoes.

Choose a high, narrow casserole with a lid and arrange the meat, onions and potatoes in layers, finishing with the potatoes and seasoning the potato layers with salt and freshly ground black pepper. Pour over enough water to come about half-way up the pot, pour over the melted butter and bake the hot pot in a moderately hot oven (400° F. Reg. 6) for 30 minutes then reduce the heat to very low (270° F. Reg. 1) and continue to cook for a further 2 hours. Remove the lid and return to a moderate oven for a final 10 minutes to brown the potatoes.

Lamb Cutlets with Cucumber and Spring Onions

There is something terribly, terribly British about lamb cutlets. To me they evoke pictures of old-fashioned clubs, decanters of port, walnuts and Stilton. For the housewife they are still good value as they are mostly lean meat, cost a realistic price and need little cooking.

Serves 4

1¼ lb best end neck lamb, *divided into cutlets*
Flour
Salt and pepper
1 egg, beaten
Dry breadcrumbs
1 oz butter
5 tablespoons olive oil
1 cucumber
12 spring onions
3 tinned tomatoes
¾ oz butter
1 teaspoon finely chopped mint
Scant tablespoon flour
¼ pint stock

Trim off any excess fat from the cutlets and trim away the meat from the long end of the bone to make a neat end. Season some flour with salt and pepper. Dip the cutlets in beaten egg, then dredge them with the seasoned flour and breadcrumbs.

Peel the cucumber, cut into four lengthwise and then into 2-inch lengths. Trim the onions, leaving 3 inches of green on the tops. Chop the tinned tomatoes.

Blanch the cucumber and onions in boiling salted water for 2 minutes and drain well. Melt ¾ oz butter in a saucepan, add the cucumber and onions and cook over a medium heat for 2 minutes. Mix in the tomatoes and simmer for 5 minutes, stirring gently every now and then. Season with salt and pepper and remove from the heat but keep warm while frying the cutlets.

Heat the oil and 1 oz butter in a frying pan until smoking. Add the cutlets and cook them for about 4 minutes on each side, turning once, until the cutlets are crisp and golden brown. Drain off excess fat on kitchen paper and keep warm. Sprinkle the flour into the juices in the pan, mix well over a high heat until flour has browned and then stir in the stock. Bring to the boil, stirring all the time, cook for 1 minute and then strain through a fine sieve.

Pile the cucumber mixture in a heated serving dish. Surround with the cutlets and sprinkle the chopped mint over the top. Serve with mashed potatoes and young, green peas.

Marinaded Leg of Lamb

A popular recipe for those who like dishes with a rich gamey flavour and with the advantage that, whereas plain roast lamb tends to be on the dreary side when cold, marinaded meat is delicious hot or cold.

> *1 leg lamb*
> *Olive oil*
> *½ pint red wine*
> *1 tablespoon sea salt*
> *1 tablespoon crushed peppercorns*
> *1 stick celery*
> *1 teaspoon thyme*
> *1 bay leaf*
> *1 small onion*
> *2 cloves*
> *Pinch allspice*

Thinly slice the celery stalk. Crush the thyme and bay leaf. Peel the onion and stick the cloves into it. Rub the leg with as much olive oil as it will absorb. Place the leg in a dish (not metal) just large enough to take it. Combine the wine, vegetables, seasoning and spices and pour them over the lamb. Marinade in a refrigerator for three days, turning the leg twice a day.

Wipe the lamb with a cloth and strain the marinade through a sieve. Place the lamb on a rack in a roasting pan, pour over the strained marinade and roast in a medium oven (325° F. Reg. 3) for 15 minutes to the pound, basting frequently, with the juices in the pan. Transfer the meat to a warm serving dish, strain the juices in the pan, leave them to settle for a couple of minutes and then skim off any fat from the surface. Serve the sauce separately.

Serve the lamb with new or roast potatoes and a good old-fashioned vegetable like glazed parsnips or cauliflower with a cream sauce. Serve a purée of chestnuts and mint or redcurrant and sage jelly on the side. *Note:* An excellent jelly to serve with hot or cold lamb can be made by combining 4 tablespoons redcurrant jelly with 2 tablespoons of mint jelly and ¼ teaspoon sage. Heat the ingredients in a saucepan until the jellies have melted. Mix well, pour into a jar and leave to set in a refrigerator.

Mutton and Mutton Broth (2 recipes)

Unfortunately mutton is all too hard to come by these days. Lamb can be used instead and although the two dishes will not have the rich strong flavour they would have had if made with mutton, the two dishes still make a nourishing main meal and substantial first course, are reasonably economical and not too arduous to prepare. Dishes like this appear in many parts of England with the ingredients varying a little from area to area. This is based on a Welsh variety which calls for the important addition of cabbage. Preparation begins a day in advance.

Each recipe serves 4–6

2 lb lower end leg of mutton or lamb
2 carrots
2 turnips
2 leeks
Quarter of a firm white cabbage
2 oz pearl barley
4 oz split peas

Pinch bicarbonate of soda
Bouquet garni
Salt and freshly ground black pepper
1 tablespoon finely chopped parsley
Water

Cover the peas with plenty of cold water and add a pinch of bicarbonate of soda. Leave to soak overnight and then drain well.

Put the meat into a large saucepan and cover with 4 pints water (spring or mineral water is infinitely preferable to mains). Bring to the boil, skim off any scum from the surface, and simmer for 1 hour. Add the pearl barley, peas and bouquet garni. Season with salt and pepper and simmer for 1½ hours.

Peel and roughly chop carrots. Peel and chop turnips. Clean and chop leeks. Add the vegetables to the meat and cook for 20 minutes. Add the cabbage, thickly shredded and cook for a further 10 minutes or until the vegetables are tender.

Transfer the meat to a heated serving dish and surround with the vegetables. Serve as a main course, sprinkling the parsley over the vegetables. Keep leftovers of meat and vegetables from the meal.

The next day cut the remaining meat and vegetables into small pieces and add to the broth from which you have skimmed all the fat. Heat through, check seasoning and serve as a substantial soup before a light main course.

Roast Lamb with Vegetables

Serves 6

3 lb shoulder or leg of lamb
Salt and freshly ground black pepper
2 cloves garlic
1½ tablespoons oil
2 rashers lean bacon
2 large onions
2 lb potatoes
½ pint good chicken stock
2 teaspoons rosemary

Peel the garlic and cut one clove into wafer-thin slithers. Remove the bacon rind and cut the rasher into equally small slithers. Using a sharp knife cut narrow slits all over the leg or shoulder of lamb

and insert the slivers of bacon and garlic into these slits. Use the
remaining clove to rub over the inside of a roasting tin. Rub the
skin of the lamb with a seasoning of salt and pepper.

Peel and thinly slice the onions and potatoes. Heat the oil in a
frying pan. Add the onions and cook over a medium heat until the
onions are transparent. Remove the onions with a slotted spoon
and reserve the juices in the pan.

Place the lamb in the centre of the roasting tin and surround
with alternate layers of onions and potatoes, seasoning each layer
very lightly with salt and pepper and a little rosemary. Pour the
juices from the frying pan and the stock over the meat and roast in
the centre of a moderate oven (350° F. Reg. 4) for 1¾ hours.

Serve the meat surrounded by the vegetables and gravy and
accompany with mint sauce or redcurrant jelly.

'Squab' Pie

Squabs usually bring baby pigeons to mind and indeed the origin
of this West Country dish was to combine pigeons with apples,
onions and potatoes. When pigeons were not available (small ones
anyway) the same pie was made with leftover mutton or lamb and
very good it is too.

According to Devonians, the pie was first made to suit the
fancies of an old farming couple who could never agree whether
squabs went better with apples or onions so they decided to combine the two. I find it is best made with crisp eating apples.

Serves 6

1 lb cooked lamb or mutton
2 tablespoons dripping
1 lb onions
1 lb crisp eating apples with plenty of flavour
¾ lb potatoes
½ pint stock
Salt and freshly ground pepper
Pinch dried thyme

Cut the lamb or mutton into small dice. Peel and chop the onion.
Peel, core and slice the apples. Peel and thinly slice the potatoes.

Heat the dripping in a frying pan. Add the onions and cook over
a medium heat until the onions are soft and transparent. Add the

apples and cook for a further 2 minutes. Lightly grease a baking dish and line it with potato slices. Cover with a thin layer of onions and apple and a layer of lamb or mutton. Season with a little salt and pepper and a suggestion of thyme and continue with the layers, finishing with a layer of potato. Pour over the stock and dribble a little of the juices from the frying pan over the potato topping. Bake in a moderate oven (350° F. Reg. 4) for 45 minutes.

Stockman's Pie

To be honest, this is really another version of the traditional Shepherd's Pie, but it is such a delicious variation that I feel no shame in including it in this collection of recipes. A long time ago, I bought a number of individual $\frac{3}{4}$-pint fireproof earthenware dishes. I find them invaluable for soup, egg dishes, pies and puddings and with recipes like these you can pre-cook and freeze the dishes without re-packing.

Serves 4

2 onions
2 tablespoons olive oil
1 lb cooked lamb or beef
2 rashers bacon
8 oz leftover cooked vegetables
(carrots, beans, peas, etc.)
1 tablespoon flour
$\frac{1}{2}$ pint stock
1 tablespoon tomato purée
1 lb potatoes
2 oz butter
Salt and freshly ground black pepper

Peel and finely chop the onions. Very finely chop the meat. Remove the rinds and finely chop the bacon rashers. Very finely chop the cooked vegetables. Peel the potatoes and cut them into wafer-thin slices.

Heat the oil, add the onions and cook until soft and transparent. Add the meat and cook quickly over a high heat until lightly browned. Add the flour, mix well and stir in the stock and tomato purée. Cover and simmer for 5 minutes and mix in the cooked vegetables. Season with salt and pepper.

Transfer the meat and vegetables to one large or four individual dishes. Cover with the thinly sliced potatoes and dribble the melted butter over. Sprinkle with a little more salt and pepper. Bake in a moderately hot oven (375° F. Reg. 5) for 45 minutes until the potatoes are crisp and nicely browned.

PORK

Fillet of Pork St John Parkes

Serves 4

¾ lb parsnips
Juice of ½ lemon
1 lb pork fillet
Salt, freshly ground black pepper
and a pinch paprika
2 tablespoons olive oil
8 ripe tomatoes
¼ pint strong stock
½ teaspoon finely chopped fresh sage
or 1 tablespoon finely chopped parsley

Peel and thinly slice the parsnips. Cover them with cold water, season with salt, add the lemon juice, bring to the boil, cover and simmer for 15 minutes. Drain well.

Trim off any fat or gristle from the pork fillets and cut the meat into ¼-inch thick slices. Flatten the slices by beating lightly with a meat mallet or rolling pin until they are about double in size. Season the slices lightly with salt, freshly ground black pepper and a little paprika. Fry them until lightly browned on both sides in hot olive oil. Drain on kitchen paper.

Cover the tomatoes with boiling water, leave to stand for 2 minutes, then drain and peel off the skins. Remove the cores of the tomatoes and roughly chop the flesh.

Arrange the pork fillet slices, sliced parsnips and tomatoes in a baking dish, pour over the stock, cover tightly with tin foil and bake in a moderately hot oven (375° F. Reg. 5) for 30 minutes. Sprinkle over the fresh sage or parsley before serving.

Home-made Pork Sausages

Much better than most shop-bought varieties. Your butcher can put the mixture in skins for you or, if you have a sausage-making attachment to an electric mixer, he should be able to supply you with skins for this purpose.

> 2 lb lean pork
> 1 lb pork belly
> ¾ lb fresh white breadcrumbs
> 2 teaspoons sage
> 1 teaspoon thyme
> Salt and freshly ground black pepper

Remove any bones or rind from the pork and pass through a mincer. Mix in the bread and herbs and season generously. Pass through the mincer again. Fry a little of the mixture to test for seasoning adding more herbs or salt and pepper if necessary. Fill skins, twisting the sausages into links at suitable intervals.

Jellied Spiced Pork

The cold table used to play a far larger part in our meals than it does now. Many of the old-fashioned cold recipes are well worth reviving and make delicious, economical meals. This country-style jellied pork is a typical example as the pork bones provide their own jelly for setting the mould.

Serves 4–5

> 1 large pork bone
> 1 large onion
> 1 bay leaf
> ½ pint chicken stock
> Salt and 8 peppercorns
> 1 lb pork fillet
> ¼ teaspoon ground ginger
> ¼ teaspoon ground cinnamon
> 1 teaspoon paprika
> Salt and freshly ground black pepper

Ask your butcher to cut the pork bone into four or five pieces. Combine the bones with the onion, roughly chopped, the bay leaf, chicken stock and peppercorns in a large saucepan. Bring to the boil, cover tightly and simmer for 30 minutes. Strain the stock through a fine sieve and remove fat when cold.

Cut the pork into very small dice and put it into a clean saucepan with the strained stock, spices and a generous seasoning of salt and freshly ground black pepper. Bring to the boil, skim off any scum from the surface, cover and simmer for $1\frac{1}{2}$ hours until the meat is fork tender. Transfer to a $1\frac{1}{2}$-pint pudding basin and leave to cool. Cover the top with a plate, weigh down with a heavy object (a large can of fruit will do) and leave in the refrigerator for at least 4 hours until set firm.

Turn out the pork, garnish with chopped cooked beetroot or watercress dipped in vinaigrette dressing and serve in slices with pickles and a fruit sauce.

Lucifer Pork Chops

Serves 4

4 pork chops
1 oz butter
1 onion
4 oz button mushrooms
4 tomatoes
1 tablespoon sugar
2 tablespoons tomato purée
1 tablespoon white or red wine vinegar
1 teaspoon mustard
Few drops Worcestershire sauce
$\frac{1}{4}$ pint water

Peel and very finely chop the onions. Finely chop the mushrooms. Peel the tomatoes by covering them with boiling water for 2 minutes and then sliding off the skins. Halve the tomatoes, remove the core and seeds (these add great flavour to a stock pot and so do the skins) and chop the flesh.

Melt the butter in a saucepan. Add the onions and cook over a moderate heat until the onion is transparent. Add the mushrooms and tomatoes and continue to cook for 2 minutes. Add the sugar, tomato purée, vinegar, mustard, Worcestershire sauce and water, bring to the boil and cook for 8 minutes.

Arrange the chops in an oven-proof serving dish, pour over the sauce and bake in a moderate oven (350° F. Reg. 4) for 45 minutes. Serve with mashed potatoes and a green vegetable.

Old-fashioned Spiced and Honeyed Pork

Serves 6

4 lb loin of pork
1 clove garlic
Salt and freshly ground black pepper
Pinch of sage, thyme, marjoram and ginger
2 tablespoons honey

Remove the skin from the pork. Peel the garlic and rub it well over the flesh of the pork. Combine salt, pepper, herbs and honey, mix well and rub the mixture over the outside of the joint. Leave in a refrigerator for at least 12 hours or overnight. Roast the pork in a moderately hot oven (400° F. Reg. 6) for 2 hours, basting occasionally. Serve with roast potatoes and apple sauce.

Pork with Cucumber in Sweet and Sour Sauce

Serves 4

1½ lb lean belly pork
1 tablespoon dripping or bacon fat
1 large cucumber
8 spring onions
1 tablespoon clear honey
1 tablespoon red or white wine vinegar
2 tablespoons strong stock
Salt and freshly ground black pepper

Remove the rind and any bones from the pork and cut the meat into ¾ inch dice. Peel the cucumber, cut lengthwise into ½-inch thick slices and then into ½-inch lengths. Chop the spring onions.

Melt the dripping or bacon fat in a frying pan. Add the pork and cook over a high heat until the meat is browned on all sides. Remove the meat from the pan with a slotted spoon. Combine the vinegar, honey and stock in a saucepan and heat through until honey is melted. Add the onions, cucumber and pork and season with salt and pepper. Cover tightly and simmer gently for about 45 minutes until pork is tender.

Pork and Onion Pudding

A nourishing and inexpensive way of making good use of belly pork providing the pork is lean.

Serves 4

> 1 lb lean belly of pork
> 1 large potato
> 2 onions
> ½ teaspoon sage
> 4 tablespoons strong stock
> Salt and freshly ground black pepper
> Extra gravy
> 8 oz self-raising flour
> 4 oz shredded suet
> Water to mix

Mix the flour and suet in a bowl. Add just enough water to make a firm dough that will form a ball and come cleanly away from the sides of the mixing bowl. Roll out two-thirds of the dough to about ¼-inch thickness and use it to line a lightly greased 2-pint pudding basin.

Remove the rind and any bones from the pork and cut the meat into small dice. Peel and coarsely grate the potato. Peel and finely chop the onions. Combine the meat, potato and onions with the sage and stock, season with salt and pepper, mix well and pack into the basin. Cover with the remaining pastry, pressing the sides firmly together.

Cover the top of the basin with two layers of greaseproof paper, a clean cloth or tinfoil, tying the sides down with string. Put the basin into a large saucepan of hot water (the water should come about three-quarters of the way up the sides of the basin) and boil for 2½ hours. Serve with extra gravy, mashed potatoes and a green vegetable.

Sausage and Cabbage Casserole

If possible choose herb-seasoned sausages (Marks and Spencer have very good ones). Never, by the way, prick sausages but cook them over a lowish heat to prevent bursting.

Serves 4

> 1 green cabbage
> 4 rashers lean bacon
> 1 quart water
> 2 sprigs parsley
> 1 sprig thyme
> 1 bay leaf
> 8 sausages
> Salt and freshly ground black pepper
> Pinch grated nutmeg
> ¾ pint beef stock

Grill or fry the sausages until well browned. Reserve the fat that comes from them while they cook.

Roughly chop the cabbage. Bring the water to the boil, add the cabbage, bacon and herbs, bring back to the boil and cook for 10 minutes. Drain well, remove the herbs and leave to cool a little. Remove the rinds from the bacon and roughly chop the rashers. Combine the bacon and cabbage, pour over a little of the sausage dripping and season with salt, pepper and a little nutmeg. Arrange half the cabbage in a lightly greased baking dish, cover with the sausages and top with remaining cabbage mixture. Pour over the stock and bake in a moderate oven (350° F. Reg. 4) for 30 minutes. Serve with mashed potatoes.

Small Raised Pork Pies

Serves 6–8

Hot-water crust pastry

> 7 fluid oz water
> 6 oz lard
> 1 lb plain flour
> ½ teaspoon salt
> 1 egg yolk

Filling

> 2 lb lean pork
> ½ lb unsmoked bacon rashers
> 2 anchovy fillets

Pinch nutmeg and allspice
1 teaspoon dried sage
Salt and freshly ground black pepper
¾ pint strongly flavoured jellied stock
1 beaten egg

To make the pastry, combine the water and lard in a saucepan and bring to the boil, cooking until the lard has melted. Add the flour, salt and egg yolk and beat hard until the dough is smooth and comes away from the sides of the pan. Leave until just cool enough to handle, cut off and reserve a quarter of the pastry to use as the pie lids. Divide up the remaining pastry, place a piece in a castle pudding or deep tartlet case and quickly push the pastry evenly around the bottom and sides of the cases forming a layer about ⅛ inch thick – the amount of pastry used in each case and the number of pies you produce depends on the size of the tins.

Chop a third of the pork into extremely small dice. Mince the remaining pork with the bacon and anchovies. Combine the diced pork with the minced ingredients, mix in the herbs and spices and season with salt and pepper. Fill the cases with this mixture, top with lids made from the remaining pastry, rolled out and cut into circles. Crimp the pastry edges very firmly together. Cut a small hole in the top of each pie. Brush with beaten egg and cut a slit in the top of each pie. Bake the pies in a moderately hot oven (400° F. Reg. 6) for 30 minutes, then lower the heat to 350° F. Reg. 4 and continue to cook for a further 45 minutes to 1 hour. Remove the pies from their tins for 5 minutes, return to the oven to brown the sides. Pour the stock into the pies through a funnel and leave to cool.

These pies are best of all when eaten slightly warm.

OFFAL

Brains in a Case

What a pity it is that brains are not more widely enjoyed in this day and age. They make delicious eating and adapt well to any manner of variations and sauces. The brains need some preparation but the flan case can be made in advance and kept chilled.

Serves 6

½ lb plain flour
Pinch salt
4 oz butter
Water for mixing (ice-cold)
1 pint stock
Bouquet garni
1 tablespoon lemon juice
1½ lb brains
6 oz mushrooms
¼ pint cream
½ oz butter
1 tablespoon flour
½ pint milk
1½ oz grated Cheddar cheese
Salt, pepper and a pinch nutmeg
1 egg yolk

Make the pastry by placing the flour and a pinch of salt in a bowl and cutting in 4 oz butter with two knives until the mixture resembles fine breadcrumbs. Add enough ice-cold water to make a stiff dough. Knead lightly, sprinkle with flour and wrap in a clean cloth. Put the pastry to chill in a refrigerator for 30 minutes and then roll out large enough to line a 9-inch flan case. Line the flan case with greaseproof paper, fill it with dried peas or beans and bake 'blind', i.e. without filling, in a hot oven (400° F. Reg. 6) for 20 minutes until golden brown.

Wash the brains under cold running water. Cover them with more cold water and leave to soak for 2 hours. Remove fibres and blanch the brains in boiling water for 3 minutes. Plunge immediately in cold water and leave until quite cold. Remove the skin and cook the brains for 30 minutes in boiling stock with the lemon juice and the bouquet garni. (The stock can be used again.) Drain the brains, leave to cool and cut into thin slices. Finely chop the mushrooms and mix them with the cream. Arrange the brains on the bottom of the flan case and spread over the cream and mushroom mixture.

Melt ½ oz butter in a saucepan. Add 1 tablespoon flour and mix well. Gradually blend in the milk, stirring continually over a medium heat until the sauce is thick and smooth. Add the cheese, season with salt, pepper and a pinch of nutmeg, bring to the boil and simmer for 3 minutes. Beat in the egg yolk and pour the sauce over the brains and mushrooms. Place under a hot grill and cook for a few minutes until bubbling and golden brown on top. *Note:* This dish can also be made with sweetbreads.

Calves' Liver Fried with Bacon

Calves' liver isn't the cheap dish it was. Nevertheless liver is rich; it can and should be cut into very thin slices and it is of a high nutritional value. The dish can be made with cheaper lamb's liver but the result is not as good.

Serves 4

1 lb calves' liver
8 rashers very thinly sliced
Streaky bacon with the rind removed
2 tablespoons olive oil
1 onion
1 tablespoon finely chopped parsley
Salt and freshly ground pepper
1 teaspoon lemon juice

Cut the liver into very thin slices and season with salt and pepper. Peel and finely chop the onion. Arrange the liver in a dish, pour over the olive oil, sprinkle the liver with the onion and parsley and leave to stand in a cool place for 2 hours.

Fry the bacon without extra fat over a medium high heat until crisp. Remove the bacon, reserving the fat in the pan, and keep the bacon warm. Scrape the onion and parsley off the liver and fry it in the bacon fat, over a very high heat, for $1\frac{1}{2}$ minutes on each side. Serve the liver and bacon with mashed potatoes and a green vegetable.

Pig's Trotters and Parsley Sauce

If you can find pig's trotters they are cheap and delicious. Ask your butcher to split them lengthwise for you.

Serves 4

4 pig's trotters
1 onion

1 carrot

1 stick celery

Salt and 6 peppercorns

½ oz butter

1 tablespoon flour

½ pint milk

2 tablespoons finely chopped parsley

1 teaspoon lemon juice

Salt and white pepper

Wash the pig's trotters and wrap them in a muslin cloth. Place them in a large pan and cover with cold water. Peel and roughly chop the onion and carrot and chop the celery. Add the vegetables to the trotters and season with salt and peppercorns. Bring to the boil, cover and simmer for 2–2½ hours. Remove the trotters, unwrap them and arrange them on a serving dish. (The stock can be used to make a rich soup.)

Melt the butter in a saucepan. Add the flour and mix well. Gradually add the milk, stirring continually over a medium heat until the sauce is thick and smooth. Add the parsley and lemon juice and season with salt and pepper. Bring the sauce to the boil and cook for 3 minutes. Pour the sauce over the trotters and garnish with extra parsley.

4
Poultry and Game

Why, oh why, did anyone think up the abomination of battery hens and the mass-produced frozen chicken; eggs with pale yolks and chickens as limp and insipid as a piece of felt? Roasting a chicken is no longer enough, these days its very leanness makes it necessary to lard and baste, its insipidness makes it essential to flavour it with herbs and spices. Still, one thing factory farming has done is to produce a cheap form of food and although it is no longer the same bird as the one that once scratched and clucked around the farmyard, today's chickens can, with imagination, be turned into reasonable meals.

Ducks, somehow, don't seem to have suffered so badly and indeed benefit from having less fat and more meat on them. I find that they can be good value and often buy two or three at a time (the 'fresh not frozen' birds from Marks and Spencer's food shops are particularly good) and keep the spares in my freezer. If you plan to serve a traditional roast duck with peas and apple sauce don't make the mistake of sweetening the apple sauce as some people do. The tartness of apple sauce makes it a good partner to duck which counteracts its fattiness, and it should be made from really tart cooking apples.

Most game is, unfortunately, expensive to buy but you can sometimes find relatively cheap old birds for casseroles and stews. These make splendid dishes and are, in fact, often preferable to a young roast bird that has been overcooked and is therefore dry and tough.

Pigeons, on the other hand, are extremely inexpensive and full of flavour but they must be eaten young. I was told the other day that the way to tell their age is by the beak; if the beak is soft and pliable, the birds will be edible. Quite how you find this out when, these days, pigeons are usually sold plucked I don't know. My only advice is to beware of flesh that is exceptionally dark and that which shows a rough texture across the breast.

Another bird that seems to be coming into its own again is the guinea fowl. These used to be popular eating up until the beginning of this century, when they seemed to disappear from the scene. Lately I have seen frozen guinea fowl in the shops again and found them very good, smaller than chickens but full of flavour with slight gamey overtones.

POULTRY

Chicken

There is great talk these days about the tastelessness of chickens. Some say this is due to the advent of the deep freeze; some that it is the fault of factory farming and the feeding of processed food rather than a handful of corn and scraps from the kitchen. I believe it is a combination of those factors, together with the inability we seem to have nowadays to hang either meat or poultry properly.

Eighteenth-century cookery books will tell you that chickens should be hung for at least two days (longer in cold weather) before being drawn and prepared for the oven. I've tried doing this with our own birds and it makes all the difference in the world; not only do the chickens have more taste but they are also much more tender. Alas, the hanging process to mature birds is almost impossible for most people to do, but I can recommend a few tips which will help to give a lift to a twentieth century chicken.

Take a tip out of our ancestors' cookery books and flavour your chickens with herbs and spices.

When in doubt about the tenderness of a bird, poach rather than roast it.

Defrost frozen chickens as slowly as possible in a refrigerator. Quick thawing ruins both the flavour and the texture of a bird.

If you can buy a fresh chicken, keep it in a refrigerator (having removed the giblets from the cavity) for 36 to 48 hours before cooking it.

Again, Marks and Spencer are to be recommended for the quality of their 'fresh not frozen' chickens.

Boiled Chicken and Broth (2 meals)

Serves 6 for each meal

1 boiling fowl
1 lemon
Water
2 lb leeks
2 chicken stock cubes
1 lb potatoes
Salt and freshly ground black pepper
Bouquet garni
2 tablespoons flour
1 oz butter
2 tablespoons double cream
1 tablespoon finely chopped parsley

Put chicken into a large saucepan with the lemon and bouquet garni. Cover with cold water, add stock cubes, bring to the boil and simmer for $1\frac{1}{2}$ hours. Remove the chicken, lemon and bouquet garni.

Clean and chop leeks. Peel and coarsely chop potatoes. Add leeks and potatoes to the stock. Bring to the boil and simmer gently until potatoes are just tender. Return the chicken to the stock with the vegetables and cook until chicken is hot through. Remove the chicken and vegetables with a slotted spoon and serve chicken and vegetables for one meal with a little of the stock as gravy.

Finely chop any remaining chicken, add it to the stock from which you have skimmed all the fat, bring to the boil and simmer for 5 minutes. Make a *roux* of the butter and flour, mixing until they are smooth. Add a little of the hot soup to make a thin sauce then stir this into the soup and bring to the boil, stirring continually until the broth is thick and rich. Add the parsley, check seasoning and blend in the cream just before serving.

Boiled Chicken with Mussel Sauce

Ideally, this dish should be made with oysters but sadly, few of these days can either afford or cope with this luxury. Mussels, on the other hand, can conveniently be bought in tins from good delicatessens (Danish mussels in $5\frac{1}{2}$-oz tins – don't be trapped into buying jars of mussels that are preserved in vinegar) and these make an excellent substitute. The delights of combining shellfish and fowl have been recognized for centuries and this is a seventeenth-century dish I would recommend highly for a twentieth-century dinner party.

Serves 6

1 roasting chicken (about 3½ lbs)
½ lemon
2 pints chicken stock or water and 1½ stock cubes
2 carrots
3 onions
3 bay leaves
2 sprigs tarragon or ¼ teaspoon dried tarragon
6 black peppercorns
5½ oz tin Danish mussels
1 oz butter
1½ tablespoons flour
¼ pint double cream
1 tablespoon finely chopped parsley
Salt and white pepper

Remove the giblets from the chicken and rub the inside with the cut side of half a lemon. Wash and thoroughly chop the carrots and cut the onions into quarters but do not remove the skins. Combine the stock, carrots, and onions, herbs and peppercorns in a saucepan large enough to take the chicken. Bring the stock to the boil and plunge in the bird, breast down. Bring back to the boil, lower the heat and simmer until the bird is tender (1–1¼ hours). Remove the bird and leave to cool for 10 minutes, then carve, cutting the breast in thick slices, separating the leg and thigh joints and leaving the wings whole. Arrange the chicken in a warm dish, cover with tinfoil and keep warm while making the sauce.

Strain the stock and skim off any fat from the surface. Strain the mussels and reserve the liquor. Melt the butter in a saucepan, add the flour and mix well. Gradually blend in ½ pint of the stock, stirring continually over a medium heat until the sauce is thick and smooth. Lower the heat, blend in the mussel liquid and the cream and season with salt and white pepper. Gently stir the mussels into the sauce, heat through and pour over the chicken. Sprinkle with a generous dusting of chopped parsley.

The dish can be covered with tinfoil and kept warm but should not be allowed to continue cooking as the mussels will then go hard and lose their fresh flavour.

Boiled Chicken with Vegetables and a Rich Sauce

Mace is an ingredient that has been widely used in English cooking for centuries, partly – in the early days – because of its preserving qualities but also for its subtle and unusual flavouring that must always be sparingly used. In the sauce that goes with this chicken and vegetable dish, mace is combined with lemon and parsley to give a superb flavour. The leftover stock will make the base for a rich and nourishing soup.

Serves 6

1 3–3½ lb boiling fowl
Water
2 stock cubes
2 parsley stalks
4 bay leaves
Salt and freshly ground black pepper
½ lemon
2 large carrots
12 small onions or shallots
1 parship
1 large leek
1½ oz butter
2 tablespoons flour
½ pint chicken stock
Juice ½ lemon
¼ teaspoon mace
2 tablespoons finely chopped parsley
3 tablespoons double cream

Place the chicken in a large saucepan, add enough cold water to cover the bird; add bay leaves, parsley stalks, ½ lemon, stock cubes and a little salt and pepper. Bring to the boil, skim off any scum from the surface, cover and simmer gently for ¾ hour. Remove the bay leaves, parsley stalks and lemon. Peel and chop the carrots and parsnip. Peel the onions and thickly slice the leek. Add the vegetables to the chicken, return to the boil and continue to simmer for a further 20–30 minutes until the vegetables and chicken are tender.

Melt the butter in a saucepan, add the flour and mix well. Gradually blend in ½ pint of the chicken stock, stirring continuously over a medium heat until the sauce is thick and smooth. Add the mace and lemon juice and mix well. Add the parsley and cream and heat through, stirring continuously until the sauce is hot but not boiling. Season with salt and pepper. Place the chicken in the centre of a heated serving dish, surround with the strained vegetables and serve the sauce separately. *Note:* Alternatively, the chicken can be carved before serving and arranged in the dish with the sauce poured over it. In this case, not all the chicken will need to be used and the remainder can go into a chicken soup.

Chicken and Bacon Rissoles

The Victorian and Edwardian housewives were masters of economy as many of their contemporary cookery books show. Unlike so many of us in these days of packaged, frozen and convenience foods of all kinds, our ancestors really knew how to make the most of small quantities of leftover meat and very delicious some of these 'reformed' dishes were.

Serves 4

3 slices white bread
10 oz cooked chicken
4 oz mushrooms
6 oz bacon rashers with rinds removed
1 egg
2 teaspoons capers
Pinch cayenne
Beaten egg and breadcrumbs for coating
Oil or lard for frying

Remove the crusts from the bread and grate the slices through a coarse grater. Mince the chicken with the mushrooms and bacon. Chop the capers very finely.

Combine the bread, chicken, mushrooms, bacon and capers, add the egg, season with a little cayenne pepper and mix well. Flour your hands and shape the mixture into thick sausage lengths about 2 inches long. Dip the rissoles into beaten egg and coat them in breadcrumbs.

Fry the rissoles in very hot lard or oil for about 8 minutes turning them frequently so that they become crisp and golden brown on all sides. Serve with Love Apple Sauce (see page 161).

Creamed Chicken with Poached Eggs

A smooth, pleasant dish that is balm to jaded palates.

Serves 4

> 12 oz cooked chicken, minced (some minced ham can
> be used to make up the quantity if necessary)
> 1 medium-sized onion
> 1 bay leaf
> 1¼ oz butter
> 1½ tablespoons flour
> ½ pint milk
> ¼ pint single cream
> Small sprig fresh tarragon (or pinch dried tarragon)
> Salt and freshly ground black pepper
> ¼ lb button mushrooms
> 4 thin rashers bacon
> 4 eggs

Peel and finely chop the onion. Remove the rinds from the bacon, roll the rashers up tightly and roast or grill them until cooked. Cool and cut into ¼-inch thick slices.

Melt 1¼ oz butter, add the onion and bay leaf and cook over a low heat until the onion is soft and transparent. Remove the bay leaf and stir in the flour. Gradually blend in the milk, stirring continually over a medium high heat until the sauce is thick and smooth. Add the minced chicken and the tarragon, cook for 2 minutes and then blend in the cream. Season with salt and pepper and spread the mixture in a serving dish. Keep warm.

Poach the eggs and drain well. Fry the mushrooms quickly in ¼ oz butter for 2 minutes only. Arrange the poached eggs, mushrooms and bacon on the minced chicken and serve at once.

Golden Chicken

Serves 4–6

> 1 3–3½ lb roasting chicken
> ¼ teaspoon cumin

$\frac{1}{4}$ teaspoon turmeric
$\frac{1}{4}$ teaspoon ground ginger
1 clove garlic
$\frac{1}{2}$ oz butter
1 tablespoon thick honey
1 teaspoon made English mustard
1 teaspoon grated finely lemon rind
Salt and pepper

Draw chicken and wipe inside and out with a damp cloth. Combine the cumin, turmeric, ginger and garlic in a mortar and pound to a paste with a pestle. Blend in the butter, honey, mustard and lemon rind and season with salt and pepper.

Rub the chicken all over with the mixture and wrap it lightly in tinfoil. Roast in a hot oven (400° F. Reg. 6) for about 1 hour until tender. Open up foil on the top for the last 10 minutes in order to give a golden crispness to the skin of the bird.

Golden Rice Croquettes Stuffed with Chicken

Despite the fact that they lived lavishly in so many ways, our Victorian forebears knew how to make a little go a long way while still producing a dish that was appetizing and well-flavoured. Leftovers were considered a challenge rather than a dirty word. These croquettes are a masterpiece; they can be served hot with a mushroom or tomato sauce or they can be left to cool and served with salad for a summer lunch or picnic.

Rice has been used in this country for centuries but, in the case of this recipe, forget everything you have learned about the importance of each grain of rice being separate. In order to keep the shape of the croquettes and their filling, the grains of rice must be soft and rather gluey.

Serves 4

6 oz long grain rice
1$\frac{1}{4}$ pints chicken stock (or water and stock cubes)
2 oz butter
8 oz cooked chicken, minced
2 hard-boiled eggs
1 onion

1 tablespoon finely chopped parsley
¼ pint rich stock or gravy
Salt and freshly ground black pepper
Small pinch cayenne pepper
1 egg
Golden breadcrumbs
Oil for frying

Bring 1¼ pints stock to the boil, add the rice and boil for 30 minutes. Beat in 1½ oz butter and continue to simmer the rice until all the moisture has been absorbed and the rice is soft. Cool. Peel and very finely chop the onion. Finely chop the hard-boiled eggs. Combine the chicken, onion and parsley with ½ oz softened butter and moisten with ¼-pint strong stock or gravy. Season with salt, pepper and a small pinch of cayenne. Cool.

To make the croquettes, place a large tablespoon of the rice in your left hand, cover with a level tablespoon of the chicken and top with a second tablespoon of rice. Using both hands, shape the croquettes, pressing the mixture firmly so that the chicken is evenly coated with rice. Chill the croquettes in a refrigerator for 30 minutes. Roll them in beaten egg and breadcrumbs and fry in ½ inch of hot oil until crisp and golden brown on all sides. Drain well on kitchen paper.

A Raised Pie of Chicken, Veal and Ham

A raised pie sounds difficult to make; but if you cheat just a little bit and use a cake tin with a removable bottom rather than attempting to do the more professional trick of raising the pie into thin air, it is quite easy to produce a really lavish pie that can make the centrepiece of a cold buffet table or provide the perfect picnic food.

The following recipe can be adapted by substituting the flesh of a pheasant or partridge for some of the chicken meat, thereby making it a game pie. Make the pie the day before you want to eat it.

Serves 10

Pastry
1 lb plain flour
6 oz lard

1 teaspoon salt
¼ pint water

Filling
1 3¼ lb roasting chicken
1 lb pork sausage meat
1 lb pie veal
¼ lb lean cooked ham
2 egg yolks
¼ teaspoon mixed dried herbs
(sage, thyme, basil)
1 onion
2 cloves garlic
1 tablespoon brandy
Salt and freshly ground black pepper
1 egg
1 teaspoon gelatine powder

To make the pastry combine the water and lard in a small saucepan and heat until the mixture boils and the lard has melted. Sieve the flour into a large basin and mix in the salt. Make a well in the centre, pour in the hot lard and water and mix lightly until the mixture forms a stiff dough. Turn on to a floured board and knead lightly to make sure the ingredients are well mixed. Place two-thirds of the pastry in a 7½-inch diameter, 3-inch high cake tin with a removable bottom and gradually press the pastry into the bottom and sides of the tin making as even a layer as possible (it is best to use your thumbs for this).

Cut off the flesh from the bird and discard the skin. Make a stock from the bones, giblets and skin. Cut the chicken breast into very thin slices and mince the rest of the flesh with the pie veal and ham. Combine the minced chicken, veal and ham with the sausage meat and egg yolks, add the onion, peeled and finely chopped, the garlic, crushed through a garlic press, herbs and brandy, season with salt and freshly ground black pepper and mix well.

Place a third of the minced mixture in the bottom of the pastry-lined tin and press down firmly. Cover with half the sliced chicken breast and repeat the process with the remaining forcemeat and chicken.

Roll out the remaining pastry to make a lid for the pie. Moisten the edges with a little water, crimp tightly together and flute the edge neatly. Brush the top with beaten egg and cut a hole in the centre of the pie. Bake in a moderate oven (350° F. Reg. 4) for $1\frac{1}{2}$ hours. Leave to cool.

Strain the stock from the chicken bones, neck and gizzard and boil it in a clean pan until it is reduced to half the quantity. Measure half a pint of stock, add the gelatine and stir until the gelatine has melted. Put a small funnel into the hole in the top of the pie and pour in as much stock as the pie will absorb. Leave to chill in a refrigerator overnight.

To turn out the pie, ease round the edges with a sharp, thin-bladed knife, invert on to a plate and gently push down on the bottom of the cake tin. Slide a knife under the bottom of the tin to remove it, place a serving plate over the pie and carefully turn it the right way up again. Serve cold, cut into thick, generous wedges.

Roast Chicken with a Rosemary Flavouring

Serves 5–6

> 1 roasting chicken (3–3½ lbs)
> Salt and freshly ground pepper
> 1 sprig rosemary
> 1 oz softened butter
> ½ pint chicken stock

If the giblets are in a plastic bag, remove them from the bag and return them to the cavity with the sprig of rosemary. Sprinkle the chicken with salt and freshly ground pepper and rub it all over with the butter. Place the chicken in a roasting dish and pour over the stock. Roast the chicken in a hot oven (400° F. Reg. 6) for $1\frac{1}{4}$ hours, basting every now and then.

Remove the chicken on to a heated serving dish and keep hot. Strain the gravy through a fine sieve, leave to settle for a few minutes and then skim off the fat from the surface. Serve the chicken with mashed potatoes and a green vegetable.

Savoury Chicken Mousse

A light, though filling, concoction which makes good use of leftover cooked chicken.

Serves 6

10 oz cooked chicken
3 rashers lean bacon
¼ pint strong chicken stock
½ oz gelatine
Salt, pepper and ⅛ teaspoon cayenne
½ pint double cream
¼ pint tinned consommé
1 teaspoon lemon juice
1 teaspoon tomato purée

Fry the bacon without extra fat over a low heat until crisp. Reserve the fat and discard the bacon rinds. Crumble the bacon rashers into small pieces. Pass the chicken twice through the fine blades of a mincer. Combine the chicken with the crumbled bacon, the bacon fat and half the stock. Season with salt, pepper and cayenne. Melt gelatine in remaining stock. Whip cream until thick. Blend gelatine mixture into chicken, mix well and fold in cream. Spoon into a glass serving bowl and chill in a refrigerator until firm.

Combine the consommé with the lemon juice and tomato purée and season with a little salt and pepper. Mix until well blended and then leave to cool. Pour over the chicken mousse and leave to set in a refrigerator. Serve well chilled. *Note:* This recipe can also be served in individual ramekin dishes as a first course.

Spiced Chicken

Herbs and spices were in common use in English kitchens from medieval times. They should never be used in excess but a subtle combination of spices can turn a mundane chicken into an exciting feast. Originally this type of recipe called for cream but I have substituted yoghurt which is less rich.

Serves 6

1 3–3½ lb roasting chicken
¼ teaspoon ground cinnamon

¼ teaspoon cardamom seeds

¼ teaspoon ground ginger

¼ teaspoon salt

4 cloves garlic

1 carton (5 oz) live yoghurt

3 teaspoons paprika

2 tablespoons olive oil

1 tablespoon flour

¼ pint chicken stock

Combine the cinnamon, cardamom seeds, ginger, salt and garlic in a pestle and mortar and grind to a smooth paste. Mix in the yoghurt.

Rub the skin of the chicken with the paprika, pour over the yoghurt mixture and leave to marinate for 2 hours. Place the bird in a roasting tin, pour over any excess yoghurt and the oil.

Roast the chicken in a hot oven (425° F. Reg. 7) for 10 minutes then lower the heat to moderate (350° F. Reg. 4) and continue cooking, basting frequently, for a further 1¼ hours or until the bird is cooked.

Remove the chicken, place in a warm serving dish and strain off the juices from the pan. Place 2 tablespoons of the juice in a small saucepan and mix in the flour. Gradually blend in the remaining juice and the stock, stirring continually over a medium high heat until the sauce is thick and smooth. Serve the sauce separately.

Stew of Duck with Anchovies

Here again the anchovy/meat combination is a winner and this recipe has the advantage of not having to be carved at the table, a job I loathe doing. Casseroling rather than roasting the bird also means that you can stretch it further.

Serves 5–6

1 duck

1½ oz butter

4 carrots

Flour for coating meat

Freshly ground black pepper

24 small shallots

4 anchovy fillets

$\frac{1}{2}$ pint brown stock
$\frac{1}{4}$ pint red wine
Bouquet garni
1 tablespoon flour
1 teaspoon lemon juice
2 tablespoons finely chopped parsley

Joint the duck and roll the joints in flour seasoned with freshly ground black pepper. Peel the shallots. Peel and slice the carrots. Heat 1 oz butter in a heavy pan, add the duck joints and brown all over. Remove the browned joints and place them in a heavy pan with the shallots, finely chopped carrots and bouquet garni. Add the stock to the juices in the pan, mix well, bring to the boil, add the wine and pour over the duck. Cover tightly and simmer for 30 minutes or until the duck is really tender (the time will depend on the age of the duck).

Remove the bouquet garni and lift out the duck and vegetables with a slotted spoon. Arrange the ingredients on a heated, shallow serving dish and keep warm. Finely chop anceovies.

Melt the remaining butter in a saucepan, add 1 tablespoon of flour and mix until brown. Gradually pour in the cooking liquid, stirring continually until the sauce is thick and smooth. Add the lemon juice, anchovies and parsley, taste for seasoning and pour over the duck. Serve with the traditional green peas and with mashed potatoes or fluffy rice.

Roast Duck with Rosemary and Marmalade Sauce

Serves 4–5

1 duck (about 4 lb)
2 oz softened butter
Salt and freshly ground black pepper
1 teaspoon rosemary
1 teaspoon finely grated lemon peel
1 onion and 1 small cooking apple
1 tablespoon flour
$\frac{1}{2}$ pint chicken stock
1 tablespoon chunky marmalade

Crush the rosemary in a pestle. Combine with the butter, season generously with salt and pepper and mix well. Rub the outside with half the butter and the inside with the remaining mixture. Peel the onion and apple and place them in the cavity. Stand the duck on a rack in a roasting tin and roast, without basting, for 40–45 minutes in a hot oven (400° F. Reg. 6). Remove the duck, place on a hot serving dish and keep warm.

Drain off all but about 2 tablespoons of the juices in the pan (keep both the fat to use as dripping for frying bread at a later date and the juices which will settle at the bottom to add richness to soups, sauces or gravy) add the flour and mix until browned.

Gradually blend in the stock, stirring continuously until the sauce is thick and smooth. Strain the gravy into a clean saucepan, mix in the marmalade and lemon peel and season if necessary with salt and freshly ground black pepper. Serve the duck with roast potatoes, cabbage and a sharp orange and watercress salad.

Poached Duck with Onion Sauce

You don't often come across boiled duck these days, especially since battery reared, ready plucked and frozen birds have virtually taken over from the much more tasty farmyard creature. It is a pity, however, to overlook this excellent recipe and, if you happen to be using a bird that may be on the old, tough side or over-fat, then this is by far the best way to treat it. The recipe also has the advantage of providing an excellent stock for soup at a later date.

Serves 4–5

1 plump duck
Coarse salt
2 tablespoons fresh sage
3 sprigs mint
3 onions

For the sauce
2 large onions
2 oz butter
1½ tablespoons flour
Pinch curry powder
½ pint chicken stock
¼ pint double cream
Salt, freshly ground black pepper and
Pinch of nutmeg

Rub the duck all over with plenty of coarse salt and leave to stand for 24 hours. Wash off the salt, soak for 30 minutes in cold water and wipe dry. Half fill a large pan with water; add the 3 onions, peeled and roughly chopped; the duck giblets, sage and mint. Bring to the boil, add the duck and cook, keeping the water just on the boil, for about 2 hours or until tender. Drain well and serve with the onion sauce and traditional green peas.

To make the sauce, peel and thinly slice the onions and separate into rings. Melt the butter in a heavy pan. Add the onions and cook over a low heat until they are soft and transparent. Add the flour and curry powder and mix well. Gradually blend in the stock, stirring continually until the sauce is thick and smooth. Bring the sauce to the boil and simmer gently for 15 minutes. Purée through a food mill, a fine sieve or in an electric liquidizer and return to a clean pan. Beat in the cream, season with salt, pepper and nutmeg and heat through without boiling.

GAME

Potted Grouse with Walnuts

One of the best ways of using a tough old bird. Although young grouse are extremely expensive to buy, especially at the beginning of the season, older stewing grouse are not exorbitant.

Serves 6

1 old grouse
1 onion
1 carrot
Bouquet garni
1 lean bacon rasher
4 juniper berries
Pinch of mace
1 wineglass sherry
Salt and freshly ground black pepper
½ pint stock
2 oz softened butter
2 oz shelled walnuts

Place the grouse in a small casserole and cover it with the bacon rasher. Peel and roughly chop the onion and carrot and surround the bird with the vegetables. Add the juniper berries (crushed), mace, sherry, bouquet garni and seasoning and pour over the stock. Cover tightly and cook in a very moderate oven (325° F. Reg. 3) for about 2 hours or until the bird is very tender. Discard the vegetables and bouquet garni, reserve the stock and leave the bird to cool.

Cut the meat off the grouse and put it through the coarse blades of a mincer with the bacon rasher. Finely chop the walnuts. Beat the butter into the minced grouse and moisten with 2 tablespoons of stock. Check seasoning, add walnuts and press the mixture into a small earthenware terrine or pot. Chill and serve with hot toast.

Braised Pigeons with Piquant Sauce

How sadly overlooked this well-flavoured bird is these days; one seldom ever sees it in the windows of butchers or poulterers, yet makes the most delicious meal for a very reasonable cost. If you deal regularly with the same butcher, he will get pigeons for you if you give him some advance warning, and if you live in London you can buy them almost all the year round from such shops as Selfridges or Harrods.

A couple of centuries ago, pigeons were kept in the stables of almost every country house. They were not particularly prized but rather were considered a useful form of supplementary food, especially for those 'below stairs'.

Although pigeons can be eaten at any time of the year, they are at their most plump in the late summer, almost bursting with the goodness of illicitly stolen corn. Young birds can be roasted, but when in doubt, casseroling is the best method of ensuring that the flesh will be tender. The compact dark meat tends to be on the dry side, so the birds need the additional lubrication of marinading, stuffing, basting and a generous wrapping of bacon to provide extra juice.

The acid flavour of plum sauce gives a delicious piquancy to the somewhat rich taste of pigeons. If you have no plum sauce, use half the quantity of H.P. or A.1 sauce.

Serves 4

4 pigeons
Flour
Salt and freshly ground black pepper
1 tablespoon olive oil
1½ oz butter
1 orange
4 rashers bacon
2 onions
4 parsnips
4 large carrots
2 tablespoons flour
¼ pint red wine
½ pint good stock
¼ pint plum sauce (see page 156)

Dip the pigeons into hot water and coat them in flour seasoned with salt and freshly ground black pepper. Peel and chop the onions. Peel and roughly chop the parsnips and the carrots.

Heat the oil and butter in a frying pan, add the pigeons and brown well on all sides over a high heat. Remove the pigeons with a slotted spoon, leave to cool a little and then stuff each one with a quarter of an orange. Wrap the pigeons in rashers of bacon from which the rinds have been removed. Add the onions, parsnips and carrots to the juices in the pan and cook over a low heat until the onions are transparent and golden brown. Remove the vegetables with a slotted spoon and spread them over the bottom of a casserole dish that is just large enough to take the pigeons.

Add the flour to the juices in the pan and mix well, stirring over a moderately high heat until the flour is lightly browned. Gradually add the stock and wine, stirring continuously over a medium heat until the sauce comes to the boil and is smooth. Season with salt and pepper.

Place the pigeons on top of the vegetables, pour over the sauce, cover tightly and cook over a low heat so that the liquid is only just moving, for 1½–2 hours until the pigeons are really tender. If you are fortunate enough to have young birds, the time for this will be considerably less. Arrange the pigeons on a serving dish. Remove the vegetables with a slotted spoon and arrange them around the birds. Keep warm.

Add the plum sauce to the juices in the casserole, mix well, adjust seasoning and bring to the boil. Strain the sauce over the pigeons and serve at once with rice or mashed potatoes and a green vegetable or salad.

Curried Rabbit

Until the war the rabbit was mainly a delicacy to be enjoyed by farmers and poachers. During the war it became a popular dish in its own right but was later removed from the market when the disease myxomatosis arrived. Today rabbits are back in the shops again, frozen and usually imported but nevertheless good value for a white, sweet meat that can be adapted to many recipes.

Serves 6

1 plump rabbit
4 onions
2 oz butter
Flour
Salt and pepper
1 tablespoon curry powder
1 tablespoon flour
About ¾ pint strong stock
Juice ½ lemon
½ lb long grain rice

Cut the rabbit into small joints. Combine some flour with salt and pepper and dust the rabbit joints generously with the mixture. Peel and roughly chop the onions.

Heat the butter in a frying pan. Add the rabbit and cook over a moderately high heat until the joints are browned on all sides. Remove rabbit, add onions to the juices in the pan and cook over a low heat until the onions are soft and transparent. Remove onions with a slotted spoon.

Add 1 tablespoon of flour and the curry powder to the juices in the pan, gradually blending in the stock, stirring continually until the gravy is thickened and smooth.

Place the rabbit and onion in a saucepan, pour over the gravy, cover tightly and simmer for 1½ hours or until the rabbit is fork tender. Check seasoning.

While the rabbit is cooking boil the rice in salted water until tender, rinse it in cold water and dry in a slow oven for a few minutes. Arrange the rice around the sides of a serving dish, pile the curried rabbit in the centre, pour over the lemon juice and garnish with chopped parsley. Serve the rabbit with any of the following garnishes:

Shredded coconut, lightly roasted in a hot oven; fried popadums, chopped cucumber in yoghurt; assorted chutneys; chopped tomatoes with a sprinkling of vinegar, salt and pepper.

5
Vegetables

Strangely, the use of vegetables in the English kitchen has decreased over the centuries. Up until the eighteenth century far more use was being made of all manner of green and root vegetables and of salads and herbs than later, when 'meat' became the overall most important item of the 'meat and two veg' syndrome. How often these days, for instance, does one eat kale greens, beet tops, salsify or seakale? Do today's housewives often choose a particular variety of potatoes for the dish they are making, and how many people now grow asparagus in their gardens?

If one is lucky enough to have a vegetable garden one can grow the most delicious and often unusual vegetables for home consumption, picking them when they are young and crisp rather than old and fibrous. Even in a small garden one can grow globe artichokes and other decorative vegetables in a border, and I know of many people who are now raising their own tomatoes, French beans and herbs in pots in a back-yard, on roof-tops, balconies or in window-boxes. It's a most satisfactory and economical process.

Now that meat and fish are becoming more and more expensive I feel we are going to join the French in having a certain number of meatless meals during the week, alternating meat or fish meals with those made of vegetables served with interesting sauces and pasta, rice or potatoes on the side. Well-cooked vegetables are an invaluable source of vitamins and minerals, and if you can combine them with an egg or cheese sauce you also provide protein for the family in meals that are both inexpensive and full of flavour.

For some time now the rage has been for imported foreign vegetables and salad stuffs and for vegetables out of season. Part of the fun, for me, about something like celery used to be that it appeared only during the winter months and then was so fresh, crisp and full of flavour. Now it seems to be around all the year, wrapped in plastic and no longer so white and crisp or so genuinely layered with rich black soil. Today it comes from as far away as Spain and California (places one would have sworn never had the all-important frost which gives celery that real crunchy texture) and all too often it is flaccid and tasteless. You can get asparagus too for a price, almost all the year round, but who wants to? The imported varieties are almost vulgarly fat and have nothing of the flavour and fresh-looking characteristics of the thinner, home-grown stalks.

Be sure to buy vegetables in their right season and make a point of asking your greengrocer for rather mundane but very worth-while items like spring greens and spring cabbage. The avail-ability of most foodstuffs is caused in the end by supply and demand and if we, the housewives, go on demanding what we want we will eventually get it. I fought hard for 'old' carrots this spring, refusing to buy those imported pale orange, suspiciously clean tasteless roots that were on sale packed in plastic bags. After constant nagging and a few eyebrows raised in surprise, my greengrocer finally got them and was amazed to find that they went like hot cakes.

For those who live in the country England has a great wealth of wild vegetables, herbs and salad ingredients in fields, hedgerows and along sea coasts. Don't overlook young nettle shoots which make a delicious soup or spinach-like vegetable, young dandelion leaves which can be used in many salads and the delicious sorrel which makes an excellent sauce.

Just because vegetables are supplementary to the main meat dish in a meal don't stint on their preparation or serving. Each vegetable should be treated as an important item in its own right and served attractively.

Bond Street Beans

Serves 4

1½ lb French beans
4 anchovy fillets
1 small clove garlic
Salt and freshly ground black pepper

Top and tail the beans and cook them in boiling, salted water until just tender.

Finely chop the anchovy fillets, reserving all the oil from the tin. Squeeze the garlic cloves through a garlic press. Combine the anchovies, oil, beans and garlic in a saucepan, season with freshly ground black pepper and heat through, stirring lightly to prevent burning. Mix well and serve at once.

East Anglian Red Cabbage

Few vegetable dishes are more suitable and complementary to game than this one. It also goes well with its traditional partner, pork.

Serves 6

1½ oz butter
1 small red cabbage
1 onion
2 cooking apples
½ gill red wine vinegar
½ gill water
2 tablespoons soft brown sugar
Salt and freshly ground black pepper

Halve the cabbage, cut out the core and shred the leaves. Well grease a baking dish with half the butter. Peel and finely chop the onion. Peel, core and thinly slice the apple. Arrange layers of cabbage, onion and apple in the casserole, sprinkling each layer with a little sugar and some salt and pepper. Finish with a layer of cabbage and dot with remaining butter. Cover tightly with tin foil and bake in a warm oven (300° F. Reg. 2) for 2 hours.

Spring Cabbage with Cream and Nutmeg

Serves 4

2 spring cabbages
½ oz butter
½ gill cream
Salt
Freshly ground black pepper
¼ teaspoon ground nutmeg

Remove the tough outer leaves of the cabbages, cut them in half and trim out the centre cores. Shred the leaves finely.

Cook the cabbages in a ½ inch of boiling, salted water until just tender but still retaining a pleasant crispness (about 5–10 minutes). Drain well.

Melt the butter in a saucepan, add the cabbage and toss lightly over a low heat until the butter is absorbed. Add the cream and season with salt, pepper and nutmeg.

Spring Cabbage Halves with Butter

Cooked properly – crisp and not mushy – this can be a delicious and attractive vegetable.

Serves 4

> 2 spring cabbages
> 1 onion
> ½ oz butter
> Salt and freshly ground black pepper

Remove the coarse outer leaves of the cabbages and cut each one in half. Neatly cut out the centre cores.

Steam the cabbage halves or cook them in a ½ inch of boiling salted water until just tender. Drain well, place in a serving dish and keep warm.

Very finely chop the onion and cook it in melted butter over a low heat, for about 3 minutes until soft and transparent. Pour the butter and onion over the cabbage and finish off with a grinding of black pepper.

White or Red Cabbage with Onions

This is equally good made with red pickling cabbage or with a firm white cabbage. Green cabbages, however, should not be used in this recipe.

Serves 4

> 2 large onions
> 1 small red or white cabbage
> 2 tablespoons dripping
> 1 oz currants
> ¼ pint rich stock
> ¼ teaspoon caraway seeds
> Salt and freshly ground black pepper

Peel and very thinly slice the onions and divide into rings. Halve the cabbage, remove the centre core and shred the leaves.

Heat the dripping in a saucepan. Add the onion rings and cook over a medium high heat until the onions are soft and golden in colour. Add the cabbage and cook over a low heat stirring continually for 2 minutes. Pour over the stock, add the currants and caraway seeds, season with salt and pepper, cover tightly and cook over a low heat, stirring occasionally to prevent burning, for twenty minutes.

Carrots – gently cooked

Serves 4

2 oz butter
¾ lb carrots
2 onions
1 oz caster sugar
1 bunch parsley
Salt and freshly ground black pepper

Peel or scrape and very thinly slice the carrots. Peel and finely chop the onion. Melt the butter in a heavy saucepan. Add the onion and cook over a low heat until the onion is soft and transparent. Add the carrots, sprinkle over the sugar and season with salt and freshly ground black pepper, cover and continue to cook over a very low heat, shaking the pan occasionally to prevent burning, until the carrots are tender (about 20 minutes). Add the parsley, check seasoning, mix lightly and turn into a heated serving dish.

'Poor Man's Asparagus'

Eaten hot with butter or cold with a vinaigrette dressing, this humble food really does taste remarkably like asparagus.

Serves 4

The outside leaves of 2 cauliflowers

Wash the leaves, spread them out and, using a sharp knife, cut out the white veins from the centre of the leaves. Trim any tough fibres from the centre of these stalks, cut them to the same length and tie them in a bundle. Cook the stalks in boiling salted water for

20–30 minutes until they are tender but still crisp. Serve them with melted butter or a vinaigrette dressing.

Cauliflower with Cucumber Sauce

Serves 6

1 medium-sized cauliflower
1 cucumber
¼ pint stock
¼ pint double cream
1 teaspoon lemon juice
1 oz butter
Salt and freshly ground black pepper

Peel and roughly chop the cucumber. Place the cucumber in a saucepan with the stock and a generous seasoning of salt and freshly ground black pepper. Bring to the boil, cover and simmer for about 15 minutes until the cucumber is tender. Purée the cucumber with the liquid in the pan through a fine sieve, a food mill or an electric liquidizer. Return to a clean pan and beat in cream, lemon juice and butter. Check seasoning and keep warm.

Steam the cauliflower over boiling water until just tender. Divide into florets and arrange in a lightly greased serving dish. Pour over the cucumber sauce and serve at once. The dish can be garnished with very tiny croutons of fried bread or with finely chopped chives or parsley.

Braised Cucumber

Serves 4

2 onions
1 cucumber
2 rashers bacon
¼ pint stock
Pinch chervil
Salt and freshly ground black pepper

Peel and chop the onions. Peel the cucumber and cut the flesh into four lengthwise and then into 2-inch lengths. Remove the rinds and most of the fat from the bacon, cut the flesh into ¼-inch strips and blanch them in boiling water for 3 minutes. Drain well.

Arrange the onions, cucumber and bacon in a fireproof baking dish, pour over the stock, add the chervil and season with a little salt and pepper. Cover tightly with tin foil and braise in a moderate oven (350° F. Reg. 4) for 30 minutes until the cucumber is transparent but not mushy.

Cucumbers in Curry Sauce

Another of those leftovers from the days of Britain's occupation of India. It goes deliciously well with chicken and fish dishes.

Serves 4

1 cucumber
1 gill double cream
1 teaspoon curry powder
Salt

Peel the cucumber and cut into neat inch-square dice. Blanch the cucumber in boiling salted water for 10 minutes until just tender.

Add the cream to the curry powder, a little at a time, stirring continually until a thin paste is formed. Combine the cucumber and the cream curry mixture in a saucepan and heat gently over a low heat, without boiling. Season with salt and simmer for 10 minutes.

Ragout of Cucumbers

A cool, delicate vegetable to serve with chicken or fish dishes.

Serves 6

2 large onions
2 cucumbers
1 oz butter
4 tablespoons gravy or strong stock
2 tablespoons white wine
⅛ teaspoon mace
Salt and white pepper
1 tablespoon flour
½ oz soft butter
2 tablespoons finely chopped parsley

Peel and very finely chop the onions. Peel the cucumber and cut the flesh into ½-inch dice.

Melt 1 oz butter in a saucepan, add the onions and cucumbers and cook over a low heat for 15 minutes, stirring occasionally to prevent browning. Add the gravy, white wine and mace, season with salt and pepper and cook for a further 2 minutes to incorporate the flavourings. Mix the flour with the softened butter to a smooth paste, stir into the ragout and cook gently over a medium heat until the sauce has thickened and is smooth and shining. Sprinkle with the chopped parsley and serve.

To prepare this dish in advance, cook as above but leave the parsley to the last minute. Cover with tinfoil and re-heat in a moderately hot oven (375° F. Reg. 5) for about 15 minutes until hot through. Sprinkle over the parsley just before serving.

Mushrooms

I think this recipe probably dates back to the eighteenth century. The combination of garlic, butter and parsley give it a flavour similar to that of snails and I find it an admirable starter before a fairly light main course. Originally it was served as a savoury, although I would have thought the garlic flavouring rather too much of a good thing at the end of a meal. Clarifying the butter gives this dish a much cleaner and purer taste.

Serves 4

> 6 oz firm button mushrooms
> 3 oz butter
> 3 tablespoons very finely chopped parsley
> 2 cloves garlic
> Salt and freshly ground black pepper
> 1 teaspoon lemon juice
> 4 thick slices of white bread with the
> crusts removed

Melt the butter in a small heavy saucepan and heat until the butter foams but does not brown. Remove from the heat and strain through a piece of muslin.

Very finely chop the garlic and add it with the parsley to the butter. Season the sauce with a little salt and plenty of freshly ground black pepper and mix in the lemon juice. Remove the stalks of the mushrooms and place the caps upside down on the slices of bread. Pour over the butter sauce and bake in a moderately hot oven (375° F. Reg. 5) for about 20 minutes. Serve at once.

Salad of Button Mushrooms and Mayonnaise

Serves 4

6–8 oz firm button mushrooms
1½ tablespoons olive oil
Juice ½ lemon
Salt and freshly ground black pepper
1 tablespoon very finely chopped parsley
1 teaspoon coarsely grated onion
¼ pint mayonnaise

Heat the olive oil in a saucepan, add the mushrooms and cook over a medium heat, shaking the pan frequently, for 10 minutes. Set aside, mix in the lemon juice, and leave to cool. Season with salt and freshly ground black pepper, and mix in the parsley and onion. Place mushrooms in a serving dish and spread the mayonnaise over the top. Chill well before serving.

Simmered Mushrooms

Commercially grown mushrooms will never have the same flavour as those picked from the fields before the sun is up – but they do have other advantages. Uniform, firm button mushrooms are available all the year round; their texture is good and they make a pleasant vegetable dish at any time of the year.

Serves 4

½ lb firm button mushrooms
¼ pint stock
2 tablespoons finely chopped parsley
1 small onion
Salt and freshly ground black pepper
1 teaspoon cider vinegar

Cut off the stalks of the mushrooms so that they come level with the caps. Peel and very finely chop the onion. Combine the stock, onion, vinegar and parsley in a small saucepan, season with salt and pepper and bring to the boil. Add the mushrooms, cover and simmer for 10–15 minutes until they have absorbed at least half of the liquid but are still pleasantly firm.

Stuffed Mushrooms

Serves 3–4

12 medium-sized, flat, firm mushrooms
(about 3 inches in diameter)
3 spring onions
2 tomatoes
2 oz lean ham
Salt and freshly ground black pepper
Fine, dry, white breadcrumbs
A little olive oil

Remove the stalks from the mushrooms. Make a stuffing by finely mincing, or very finely chopping, the mushroom stalks, trimmed spring onions, the peeled tomatoes and the ham with all the fat removed. Season the mixture with salt and freshly ground black pepper. Spread the stuffing evenly on the stalk side of the mushroom caps, covering them completely. Sprinkle over a very thin layer of breadcrumbs and brush with a little olive oil. Grill under a medium flame until golden brown. These can be served cold or re-heated.

Parsnips and Onions

This good vegetable dish takes a lot of beating. As the parsnips are a root vegetable and therefore relatively starchy, don't serve potatoes as well. A mixed salad makes a good second side dish if the vegetable is to be served as a main course.

Serves 6

1½ lb parsnips
Juice of ½ lemon
2 large onions
2 oz butter
¼ pint milk
Salt and freshly ground pepper
1 tablespoon finely chopped parsley

Peel the parsnips, cut lengthways into thin strips and put them at once into cold water to which the juice of a ½ lemon has been added. Peel and very thinly slice the onions.

Grease a baking dish and arrange the parsnips and onions in layers, seasoning each layer with salt and freshly ground black pepper. Pour over the milk and dot with the butter cut into small pieces. Cover tightly with tinfoil and bake in a moderately hot over (375° F. Reg. 5) for 45 minutes. Remove the cover, spoon some of the liquid over the top of the vegetables and return to the oven for a further 15 minutes. Sprinkle with finely chopped parsley before serving.

Purée of Seasoned Parsnips

We all know people who say they hate parsnips, but serve them this dish and I guarantee they will change their minds.

Serves 4

1½ lb sound parsnips
1 teaspoon lemon juice
2 oz butter
1 onion
½ pint milk
Salt, pepper and ¼ teaspoon nutmeg

Peel and roughly chop the parsnips and cook them in boiling salted water with the lemon juice until tender. Drain them well and mash until smooth or purée through a sieve, food mill or electric liquidizer.

Peel and finely chop the onion and cook it in the butter over a low heat until the onion is soft and transparent. Add the parsnip purée and mix well. Gradually blend in the milk, a little at a time, beating continually with a wooden spoon so that the milk is completely absorbed by the parsnips. Beat in the nutmeg and season with salt and pepper. Serve piping hot.

Rich Panned Potatoes

Serves 4

1½ lb potatoes
2 rashers streaky bacon

1 onion
2 egg yolks
Salt and freshly ground black pepper
Dripping or bacon fat for frying

Peel the potatoes and boil them in salted water until tender. Mash
the potatoes until smooth and leave to cool a little.

Remove the rinds from the bacon and finely chop the rashers.
Peel and finely chop the onion. Heat a little dripping in a frying
pan, add the bacon and onion and cook over a medium heat until
the onion is soft and transparent. Beat the egg yolks into the
mashed potato and mix in the bacon and onion. Season with salt
and pepper.

Heat a little dripping in a heavy frying pan, slide pats of the
potato mixture into the pan from a large spoon and flatten them to
about ½-inch thickness. Cook over a high heat until well browned
underneath, then turn over and brown the other side. Drain on
kitchen paper.

Sorrel – The Roman Way

Sorrel is another of those old-fashioned vegetables that most
people overlook these days. The bitter-sweet taste makes sorrel
an exciting vegetable to serve with a plain dish such as roast
chicken or grilled fish; young leaves make an excellent addition
to summer salads and sorrel can also form the base of an unusual
sauce. Sorrel can also be used in place of, or as well as, chervil or
parsley as additional flavouring for vegetable soups.

The Romans were the first to cultivate sorrel in order to increase
the flavour of the plant and, according to Pliny, the following
method of cooking the leaves was extremely popular. If sorrel is
not available, spinach can be cooked in the same way and the end
result is a sort of hot salad which I find goes well with almost any
plain dish.

Unfortunately, it is difficult to find sorrel on sale in the average
city greengrocer but those who live in the country can pick it for
free in the fields; and if you find you acquire a taste for 'rumex
acetosa', it is an easy plant to grow in either a vegetable patch or
a flower garden.

Serves 4–6

1½ lb fresh sorrel or spinach
2 teaspoons French Dijon mustard
4 tablespoons olive oil
1 tablespoon white wine vinegar
Salt and freshly ground black pepper

Remove any tough stalks from the leaves and cook the sorrel or spinach in plenty of boiling, salted water until tender. Drain well. Mix the mustard with the oil and vinegar. Return the leaves to a clean pan, add the vinaigrette dressing, season with salt and a generous screw of black pepper and toss lightly over a medium heat until hot through.

Turnip Cooked with Onions in Stock

Many people claim to dislike the taste of swedes or turnips but I wonder if they have ever had them really well prepared. This method with turnips is delicious and goes well with any fairly plain main course.

Serves 4

1 medium-sized turnip
1 tablespoon dripping
1 large onion
½ pint rich stock
Salt and pepper
2 tablespoons finely chopped parsley

Peel the turnip and then cut it into ¼-inch thin slices. Cut the slices into sticks about ½ inch wide and 2 inches long. Peel and thinly slice the onion and separate the slices into rings.

Heat the dripping in a heavy pan. Add the onion rings and cook over a medium low heat until the onion is soft and transparent. Add the turnip, mix well and continue to cook, stirring every now and then, for about 5 minutes until all the fat has been absorbed. Pour over the stock, season with salt and pepper, bring to the boil, cover and simmer gently for about 40 minutes until most of the stock has been absorbed and the turnip slices are almost transparent and rather waxy. Gently drain off any excess stock, arrange the onion and turnip on a heated serving dish and sprinkle over the chopped parsley just before serving.

SALADS

Dandelion and Bacon Salad

Springtime dandelion leaves, when picked young, have only a trace of bitterness which is, in fact, rather pleasant. Here are two versions of old-fashioned salads utilizing these very ordinary weeds.

Serves 4

1 quart young dandelion leaves
4 rashers streaky bacon
3 tablespoons olive oil
½ teaspoon mustard
1 tablespoon white wine vinegar
Salt and freshly ground black pepper
½ teaspoon sugar

Wash the leaves, dry them well and arrange them in a bowl. Cut the bacon into small pieces and fry without extra fat until crisp. Drain on kitchen paper and sprinkle over the dandelion leaves.

Combine the oil with the mustard and vinegar, season with salt and pepper, add the sugar and mix well. Pour over the dressing and toss the salad lightly before serving.

Wilted Dandelion Salad

Serves 4

1 lb young dandelion leaves
6 thin rashers streaky bacon
1 tablespoon olive oil
1 clove garlic
1 tablespoon finely chopped parsley
2 tablespoons finely chopped mint
Salt and freshly ground black pepper
½ gill red wine vinegar

Remove the rinds and finely chop the rashers. Crush the cloves of garlic through a garlic press. Heat the olive oil, add the bacon and garlic and cook over a medium heat until the bacon is crisp.

Remove from the stove, mix in the vinegar, mint and parsley and season with salt and pepper.

Wash the dandelion leaves and dry well. Pour the dressing over the dandelion leaves while it is still warm and toss lightly.

English Tomato Salad

Although I do use tinned tomatoes for cooking, there is nothing to beat a good English tomato for salad flavour.

Serves 4

¾ lb firm tomatoes
6 spring onions
1 crisp lettuce
4 tablespoons olive oil
4 tablespoons tarragon vinegar
Salt and freshly ground black pepper

Cover the tomatoes with boiling water for 2 minutes and then slide off the skins. Cut the tomatoes into thin slices. Trim the onions and chop them finely. Remove the outer leaves of the lettuce and separate the leaves of the heart. Line a salad bowl with the heart leaves and place the tomatoes in layers in the centre, sprinkling the spring onions and a little salt and pepper over each layer.

Combine the oil and vinegar and mix well. Pour the dressing over the tomatoes and chill in the refrigerator before serving.

Old English Salad with Lemon Verbena

Serves 4

1 Cos lettuce
1 Webbs Wonder lettuce
1 head endive
Small sprig lemon verbena
½ tablespoon finely chopped parsley
1 tablespoon finely chopped chives
10 small spring onions
¼ teaspoon dry mustard
¼ teaspoon sea salt
Good pinch cayenne
2 tablespoons olive oil
Scant tablespoon with white wine vinegar

Use only hearts of lettuces and endive. Clean hearts and break into small shreds with your fingers. Strip the lemon verbena leaves from the stalk and finely chop the leaves. Remove all the green part of the spring onions and trim and chop the bulbs. Place the chopped bulbs in a basin with the mustard, salt, cayenne and oil; mash with a fork until very well blended. Blend in the vinegar and mix thoroughly. Add the chives, verbena and parsley to the dressing. Combine the lettuces in a salad bowl, pour over the dressing and toss lightly before serving.

6
Luncheon and Supper Dishes

This chapter is made up of a wide selection of recipes, many of which might have been classified in the nineteenth century as high tea or even breakfast dishes. Breakfast, for instance, for the Georgians, Victorians and even the Edwardians was one of the major meals of the day and often included such dishes as devilled kidneys or chicken legs, marinated fish or potted meats. As breakfast is no longer in fashion and high teas are rapidly being replaced by a movable feast called 'supper' I have placed in this section those recipes which do not fit into the other main categories, and I leave it to you to decide when to produce them for family meals.

British cooking owes a lot to those two meals of breakfast and high tea and a lot of recipes which had their places on the menus for those particular meals are now in danger of being forgotten. The recipes in this section will, I hope, play their part in restoring them to a place worthy of their value.

Also included in this section are some of the wartime recipes which came into their own in the 1940s and which have since been forgotten; recipes which made the best possible use of locally grown produce and which provide nutritiously valuable meals at a very budget-conscious price. With inflation ever present I think we are going to have to rely on this kind of frugal cooking a great deal more. Thrift often brings out the best in a cook and it is surprising how often it is the well-thought-out dish rather than the more exotic, luxury-priced concoction that brings the enjoyment.

In this section you will also find dishes to suit housewives who have a career as well as managing and cooking for a family; quickly prepared food that tastes good but does not need hours of preparation, and can be served when it is needed.

BACON RECIPES

Bacon Floddies

Serves 4

½ lb potatoes
2 onions
2 eggs
2 oz self-raising flour
6 oz lean bacon rashers
Salt and freshly ground black pepper
Dripping or lard for frying

Peel and coarsely grate the potatoes and onions. Remove the rinds from the rashers and very finely chop or mince the bacon. Beat the eggs and add them, with the bacon, to the potatoes and onions. Sprinkle over the flour, season with salt and pepper and mix well.

Heat a little dripping or lard in a frying pan, add the floddie mixture in tablespoonfuls and cook until golden brown on both sides. Drain on kitchen paper. These can be served as a vegetable, as a main course with fried eggs or as a supper dish on their own.

Bacon and Cheese Custard Pie

Can be served hot or cold.

Serves 4

6 oz shortcrust pastry
2 eggs
½ pint milk
4 oz Cheddar cheese grated
Salt and pinch cayenne
½ tablespoon finely chopped green pepper
4 thin rashers streaky bacon

Roll the pastry out thinly and line a 7-inch flan case. Beat the eggs until smooth, beat in the milk and mix in the cheese and green pepper. Season with salt and a little cayenne.

Remove the rinds from the rashers and cook the bacon without extra fat over a medium heat for about 4 minutes. Drain rashers on kitchen paper and cut into 1-inch pieces.

Arrange the bacon in the bottom of the flan case. Pour over the cheese custard and bake in a moderately hot oven (375° F. Reg. 5) for 30 minutes or until the custard is nicely set and the top golden brown.

Bacon and Eggs

Why bother to include anything so mundane in a cookery book, you might wonder. Well, the answer is that this isn't just any old way of cooking the traditional Englishman's breakfast. Eggs and bacon cooked together this way have a very special flavour as well as looking far more attractive than the frequent flabby rasher and staring fried egg.

Serves 4

4 thin rashers streaky bacon
4 eggs

Remove the rinds from the bacon and cut the rashers into small pieces. Fry over a low heat until most of the fat has melted and the bacon is crisp without being burnt. Remove the bacon from the pan with a slotted spoon. Strain the fat.

In a clean pan (preferably a non-stick frying pan) heat 1 table-spoon of the strained bacon fat. Add a quarter of the bacon pieces, spreading them over a circle about 4 inches in diameter and break over an egg. Cook over a moderately low heat until the white of the egg is just set. Remove the egg and keep warm while cooking the other three in the same way.

Bacon and Egg Pie

My helpmate, Julie, makes delectable egg and bacon pies for suppertime or picnics. Her secret is the lavish use of parsley.

Serves 4–5

8 oz plain flour
4 oz butter
Salt and white pepper
Water to mix
8 oz lean bacon rashers
4 eggs
¼ pint double cream

2¼ *tablespoons parsley*
Salt, pepper and a pinch of nutmeg

Put the flour into a bowl with a little salt and pepper. Add the butter cut into small pieces and rub the butter into the flour until the mixture resembles coarse breadcrumbs. Add just enough cold water to make a firm dough and knead lightly until smooth. Wrap in a floured cloth and refrigerate for 20–30 minutes. Line a flan tin with half the pastry, rolled out thinly.

Remove the rind from the bacon and cut the rashers into 1-inch pieces. Arrange the rashers in the case and break over the eggs. Combine the cream with the parsley, season with salt, pepper and a pinch of nutmeg and pour this over the eggs. Cover the pie with the rest of the pastry, pinch the edges together firmly, brush with beaten egg and make a slit in the centre. Use any remaining pastry to make a pattern of leaves on the top. Bake in a hot oven (400° F. Reg. 6) for about 30 minutes until the pastry is cooked and golden brown. Serve warm or cold.

Leek and Bacon Dish

From Wales come countless dishes that incorporate leeks with other vegetables or bacon to make first-rate lunch or supper dishes.

Serves 4

1½ *lb fat leeks*
1 chicken stock cube
8 oz bacon rashers
1 oz butter
1 oz flour
1 tablespoon finely chopped Piccalilli
Pepper

Wash leeks well and cook them in boiling water, to which a stock cube has been added, for about 20 minutes or until just tender. Reserve the cooking liquid. Drain well by placing them upside down in a colander and then arrange them in a fireproof baking dish.

Remove the rinds from the bacon and chop the rashers. Melt the butter in a saucepan, add the rashers and cook until crisp. Stir in the flour and gradually blend in ½ pint of the cooking liquid, stirring continually until the sauce is thick and smooth. Add the piccalilli. Season with pepper, pour the sauce over the leeks and reheat in a moderate oven (350° F. Reg. 4) for about 15 minutes. Serve with potatoes baked in their jackets.

Penwith Bacon and Onion Tart

An old-fashioned open savoury tart that has a touch of saffron, an ingredient that is still extremely popular in Cornish cookery.

Serves 4

Pastry
6 oz flour
3 oz butter
1 small egg
1 oz Cheddar cheese (finely grated)
½ teaspoon salt
About 2 tablespoons cold water

Filling
1 oz butter
2 large onions
4 rashers bacon (approx. 4 oz)
3 eggs
Salt and pepper
¼ pint double cream
¼ teaspoon saffron
2 oz raisins

To make the pastry sieve the flour with the salt into a bowl. Add the cheese and the butter cut into small pieces and, using two knives or a pastry cutter, cut the butter into the flour until the mixture resembles fairly firm breadcrumbs. Add the egg and mix well. Mix in enough cold water to make a stiff dough, wrap in a clean cloth and leave in a refrigerator for about 30 minutes before rolling out. Roll the pastry out thinly and line a 9-inch flan case. Leave the case to chill in the refrigerator until the filling is made. For the filling peel and very thinly slice the onions. Remove the rinds from the bacon and cut the rashers into thin strips. Heat the butter in a frying pan, add the onions and cook over a medium low heat for about 3 minutes until the onions are soft and transparent.

Infuse the saffron in the cream and heat over a low heat to just below boiling point. Remove from the heat and leave to cool for about 10 minutes. Beat the eggs, add the cream and mix to a custard consistency. Add the raisins and season with salt and pepper.

Arrange the onions and bacon in the bottom of the flan case and pour over the custard mixture. Bake in a pre-heated hot oven (400° F. Reg. 6) for 10 minutes then lower the heat to moderate (350° F. Reg. 4) and continue to cook for a further 20 minutes or until the custard is just set. Serve hot or cold with salad.

CHEESE RECIPES

Cauliflower Cheese as a Main Course

Serves 4

1 cauliflower
1 onion
1½ oz butter
4 oz lean ham
2 tomatoes
2 tablespoons flour
½ pint milk
1 teaspoon English made mustard
2 egg yolks
4 oz grated Cheddar cheese
Salt, pepper, pinch cayenne

Steam the cauliflower until tender (or cook it in a little boiling salted water and drain well). Cool and divide into florets. Peel and very finely chop the onion. Chop the ham. Peel the tomatoes (plunge them into boiling water for 2 minutes and then slide off the skin) and chop the flesh.

Melt the butter in a saucepan, add the onion and cook over a low heat until the onion is soft and transparent. Add the flour and mix well. Gradually blend in the milk, stirring continuously over a medium heat until the sauce is thick and smooth. Add half the cheese and continue to stir until the cheese has melted. Lower the heat and beat the egg yolks into the sauce. Do not boil. Season with salt, pepper and a pinch of cayenne, lightly fold in the cauliflower, tomatoes and ham and transfer to a fireproof serving dish. Sprinkle over the remaining cheese and cook in a moderate oven (350° F. Reg. 4) for 15–20 minutes until the dish is hot through and the top is golden brown.

Crisp-topped Cauliflower Cheese

Serves 4

> 1 medium-large cauliflower
> 1½ oz butter
> 1 medium-sized onion
> 2 tablespoons flour
> ½ pint milk
> 1 teaspoon made mustard
> 2 oz ham
> 3 oz grated cheddar cheese
> 2 oz fresh white breadcrumbs
> 1 oz melted butter
> Salt and freshly ground black pepper

Steam the cauliflower over boiling water for about 20 minutes until just tender but still crisp. Cool and divide into florets. Arrange the florets in a lightly greased baking dish. Peel and very finely chop the onion. Finely chop the ham.

Melt 1½ oz butter in a saucepan, add the onion and cook over a low heat until the onion is soft and transparent. Add the flour and mix well. Gradually blend in the milk, stirring continuously over a medium high heat until the sauce is thick and smooth. Add the mustard and cheese and continue to stir over a low heat until all the cheese has melted. Mix in the ham and season with salt and freshly ground black pepper. Pour the sauce over the cauliflower.

Brown the breadcrumbs in a hot oven (400° F. Reg. 6) for 2–3 minutes until they are a pale golden brown. Scatter the breadcrumbs over the cauliflower cheese and dribble the melted butter over the breadcrumbs. Heat through in a moderate oven (350° F. Reg. 4) for about 20 minutes until the dish is bubbling.

Stilton Soufflé

Stilton is one of the best of our traditional British cheeses but, like all good things, it is sometimes possible to have too much. Recently, one of my guests for a weekend party arrived bearing half a superbly ripe Stilton, a generous and lovely present. The only problem was that I had already bought an equally large portion myself. With such a surfeit of cheese, I became an expert in producing Stilton-based dishes, one of the most successful of which was the following soufflé which can be served either as a first course or as a savoury course. With a soufflé timing is all-important. Ideally, the dish should be crisp on the outside, yet still soft and moist (almost runny) in the centre. If you feel your soufflé is cooked before your guests are ready for it, leave it in the oven and turn off the heat. Soufflés are far less sensitive than many people would have you believe and by following the above method I have kept soufflés 'on ice', so to speak, for as long as 15 or 20 minutes.

Serves 4

1 oz butter
1 tablespoon flour
1 teaspoon made English mustard
¼ pint milk
4 oz Stilton cheese
Salt, pepper and a pinch cayenne
3 eggs, separated
A little extra butter

Pre-heat oven to moderately hot (375° F. Reg. 5). Crumble the Stilton. Beat egg yolks until smooth. Melt the butter in a saucepan. Add the flour and mustard and mix well. Gradually add the milk, stirring continually over a medium heat until the mixture comes to the boil and is thick and smooth. Add the Stilton and simmer, stirring over a low heat until all the cheese has melted and been incorporated. Remove from the heat and leave to cool for 2 minutes. Beat in the egg yolk a little at a time and season with salt, pepper and a pinch cayenne.

Whip the egg whites until stiff and fold them lightly into the soufflé base (a wire whisk – not the rotary kind – is the best implement for this).

Lightly grease four individual soufflé dishes (or one large one) and bake in a hot oven (400° F. Reg. 6) for 20 minutes for individual soufflés or 30 minutes for a large one. The soufflés should be well risen with a golden brown, crisp topping.

Welsh Rarebit

There are so many ways of making this savoury that it is hard to choose which one is really the best, but it does seem certain that the authentic Welsh variety was traditionally made with brown ale.

Serves 4

6 oz finely grated Cheddar cheese
1½ oz butter
¼ gill brown ale
Salt and white pepper
¼ teaspoon mustard
Small pinch cayenne
4 slices hot buttered toast

Melt the butter. Add the cheese, ale, mustard and seasoning and cook over a very low heat, stirring continually, until the cheese has just melted. Over cooking will give a stringy effect. Spread at once on the toast.

Welsh rarebit can make a good supper or luncheon dish if served with crisply fried streaky bacon and grilled tomatoes.

EGG RECIPES

Brunch Omelette

This was a popular post-World War II dish. Whether it was served as a breakfast or high tea speciality I am not quite sure, but I do know, from practice, that it makes an ideal quick luncheon or supper recipe and is delicious served with a fresh green salad.

Serves 4

4 streaky rashers bacon with the rinds removed
1 thick slice bread with the crusts removed
4 eggs
Salt, pepper and ⅛ teaspoon English mustard powder
¼ oz butter

Cut the bacon into very small dice. Cut the bread into small dice. Fry the bacon, without additional fat, over a low heat until it is crisp. Remove the bacon from the pan with a slotted spoon and drain it on kitchen paper. Fry the bread cubes in the bacon fat until golden brown on all sides. Drain on kitchen paper and keep both the bacon and bread cubes warm while making the omelette.

Combine the eggs with a little salt and pepper and the mustard. Beat lightly with a wire whisk. Heat the butter in an omelette pan, pour in the egg mixture and cook over a medium high heat, raising the edges of the omelettes with a spatula to let the uncooked egg slide underneath. When the omelette is just set firm (but not dry) sprinkle the bacon and bread cubes along the centre. Fold the omelette in half and slide on to a heated serving dish. Serve at once.

Curried Eggs

Normally this dish is served hot with rice as a good economical supper dish, but it is also delicious cold. Some of the best memories I have of food are of hunts in Ireland just before I was married. The hunt itself used to terrify me but the picnic we had in the horse-box before going home made it all worth while: delicious curried eggs, eaten with a spoon and washed down by a warming mixture of half port, half brandy – I strongly recommend it as one of the best possible picnic combinations.

Serves 4

8 eggs
2 tablespoons olive oil
2 onions
1 tablespoon curry powder
1 tablespoon flour
¾ pint chicken stock
1 tablespoon apricot jam
1 tablespoon mango chutney
3 slices lemon
3 tomatoes

Hard boil the eggs for 8 minutes, plunge them into cold water and remove the shells. Peel and very thinly slice the onions. Finely chop the mango chutney and the slices of lemon. Cover the tomatoes with boiling water for 2 minutes then peel off the skins; remove the core and seeds and finely chop the flesh.

Heat the oil in a heavy saucepan. Add the onions and cook over a low heat until the onions are soft and transparent. Add the curry powder, mix well and continue to cook for 2 minutes until the curry powder is well coloured. Blend in the flour and gradually stir in the stock. Bring the sauce to the boil, mix in the tomatoes, chopped lemon, chutney and jam and simmer for 30 minutes.

Halve the eggs and place them, cut side down, in a serving dish. Pour over the sauce and leave to cool. If the dish is to be served hot, reheat in a moderately hot oven and serve with fluffy boiled rice.

Egg Croquettes

Apart from making a delicious first course when served with a spicy tomato sauce, these croquettes also provide good picnic material when served cold. Use home-made breadcrumbs rather than packaged. They can be made by drying stale slices of bread in a very low oven until crisp, then crushing into fine crumbs with a rolling-pin.

The croquette mixture will be easier to handle if it is made some time in advance and allowed to chill thoroughly.

Serves 4

> 1½ oz butter
> 3 tablespoons flour
> 1½ gills milk
> Slice raw onion
> 1 bay leaf
> Pinch mace
> 5 peppercorns
> 4 hard-boiled eggs
> 1 tablespoon finely chopped parsley
> Few drops Tabasco sauce
> 1 egg yolk
> Salt and pepper
> 1 beaten egg
> Dried white breadcrumbs
> Deep fat or oil for frying

Combine the milk, onion, bay leaf, mace and peppercorns in a saucepan, bring to the boil and simmer gently for 20 minutes. Strain. Melt the butter in a clean pan, add 3 tablespoons flour and mix well. Gradually blend in the strained milk, stirring continually,

until the sauce comes to the boil and is very thick and smooth.
Add egg yolk and beat well.

Chop the hard-boiled eggs and add to the sauce with the parsley
and tabasco. Season with salt and pepper and mix well. Chill the
mixture until firm.

Divide into large spoonfuls and shape into 2-inch long fat
sausage shapes on a floured board. Beat the egg with a little salt.
Dip the croquettes in the egg and then roll them in the breadcrumbs. Heat the fat or oil until smoking, carefully immerse the
croquettes and cook until crisp and golden brown. Remove with a
slotted spoon and drain on kitchen paper.

Eggs with Ham on Macaroni

Much more sophisticated than macaroni cheese and very delicious.

Serves 4

4 eggs
4 thin slices ham
3 oz macaroni
2¼ oz butter
2 tablespoons flour
¾ pint milk
1 small onion
1 bay leaf
Bouquet garni
2 oz grated Cheddar cheese
Salt and pepper

Combine the milk with the onion, bay leaf and bouquet garni,
bring to the boil and simmer gently for ½ hour. Strain.

Cook the eggs in boiling water for 5 minutes. Plunge immediately in cold water and peel carefully.

Cook the macaroni in boiling, salted water until tender. Drain,
toss in 1 oz butter and spread over the bottom of a fireproof serving
dish. Wrap each egg in a slice of ham and place them on the
macaroni; keep warm while making the sauce.

Heat the remaining butter in a saucepan, add the flour and mix
well. Gradually blend in the milk, stirring continually until the
sauce comes to the boil and is thick and smooth. Add 1½ oz cheese,
stir until the cheese has melted, then pour the sauce over the eggs.

Top with remaining cheese and brown quickly under a hot grill until cheese is bubbling and golden.

Eggs Tremaine

This is an old recipe that I pinched from the menus of one of the most beautiful houses in England. Serve it as a sensational first course or double the quantities to serve as a luncheon or supper dish. The eggs should be between soft and hard-boiled and cooked for no longer than 5 minutes.

Serves 4

4 eggs
3 oz long grain rice
1 tablespoon cream
Salt and cayenne
2 egg yolks
1 shallot or small onion
4 tablespoons white wine vinegar
Pinch mace
Pinch thyme
3½ oz softened butter
3 tablespoons boiling water

Boil the eggs for 5 minutes. Plunge them immediately in cold water and leave to cool. Carefully remove the shells.

Boil the rice in salted water for 20 minutes or until tender, drain in a sieve and rinse under cold running water. Drain well, mix with the cream and ½ oz of the butter and season with a little salt and cayenne. Divide the rice between four lightly buttered ramekin dishes, pressing it in firmly and making a slight depression in the centre in which to place the eggs. Cover the dishes with a layer of kitchen foil.

Peel and very finely chop the shallot and combine it with the vinegar and herbs in a saucepan. Bring to the boil and cook over a high heat for about 5 minutes until the vinegar has all been absorbed into the shallot. Then beat the egg yolk until smooth, blend in the shallot and remaining softened butter. Cook over a very low heat (or in a double boiler), beating all the time until the sauce is smooth, thick and emulsified. Remove from the heat and beat in the boiling water a little at a time.

Heat the ramekins through in a moderately hot oven (350° F. Reg. 4) for 5 minutes or until hot through. Remove the foil, pour over the sauce and serve at once. *Note:* If the sauce curdles after cooking don't worry. The addition of the boiling water should return it to a thick creamy consistency.

Macaroni Pudding

Macaroni was extremely popular with the Victorian housewife and was used as the basis of many budget-conscious dishes. This 'pudding' variation beats the common or garden macaroni cheese into a cocked hat.

Serves 6

¼ lb macaroni (use the genuine
Italian macaroni if possible)
1 tablespoon salt
5 egg yolks
2 egg whites
½ pint single cream
¼ lb cooked chicken or ham or half of each
3 tablespoons Parmesan cheese
Salt and white pepper

Break the macaroni into pieces roughly 1½ inches long and cook it in boiling water with a tablespoon of salt until just tender (about 15 minutes), drain well, rinse in cold water and drain again.

Cut the cooked chicken or ham into small dice. Beat the eggs with the cream, add the Parmesan, season with salt and pepper and mix well, adding the meat.

Generously butter a pudding basin, fill with the macaroni, pour over the egg mixture and cover tightly with foil. Place the basin in a large saucepan with enough water to come half-way up the sides of the basin and boil for 1 hour and 15 minutes. Turn out and serve at once with Love Apple Sauce (see page 161).

Stuffed Eggs with Parsley Sauce

Serves 4–6

8 eggs

3 tomatoes

1 small onion

½ tablespoon olive oil

3 anchovy fillets

Milk

Pinch dried sage and basil

1 tablespoon finely chopped parsley

Pinch thyme

Freshly ground black pepper

Sauce

1 chicken stock cube

½ gill boiling water

2 oz butter

1½ tablespoons flour

¼ pint milk

¼ pint cream

2 tablespoons finely chopped parsley

Hard-boil eggs, rinse in cold water, shell and cut in half length-ways. Remove the yolks and mash to a smooth paste. Peel the tomatoes (cover them with boiling water for 2 minutes and slip off the skin), remove the cores and seeds and finely chop the flesh.

Soak the anchovy fillets in milk for a few minutes to remove excess salt. Squeeze dry and very finely chop fillets. Finely chop onion, cook over a low heat in the oil until soft and transparent. Add tomatoes and continue to cook for 5 minutes. Remove from the heat and blend the mixture into the egg yolks. Add the anchovies and herbs and season with pepper. Stuff the egg whites with this mixture and place them flat side down in a fireproof serving dish.

To make the sauce dissolve the stock cube in the boiling water. Melt the butter in a saucepan over a medium heat. Add the flour and mix well. Gradually blend in the stock and milk, stirring con-tinually until the sauce is thick and smooth. Lower heat and stir in the cream and parsley, season the sauce with pepper (add a little extra milk if the sauce is too thick) and pour over the eggs. Cover with foil and heat through for about 10 minutes in a moderately hot oven (375° F. Reg. 5). Serve with hot toast and butter.

FRUIT AND VEGETABLE RECIPES

Apple and Cheese Pie

The apple/cheese combination is always a popular and satisfactory one. In this recipe the two ingredients are combined in an old-fashioned savoury tart which goes extremely well with a bit of boiled bacon or crisply fried rashers of bacon and sausages. It can be served warm or cold.

Serves 4

> 6 oz flour
> ¼ teaspoon salt
> 3 oz butter, margerine or half butter and lard
> 1 small egg
> Water to bind
> 1 small onion
> ¼ oz butter
> 1½ lb cooking apples
> 1½ tablespoons sugar
> 6 oz coarsely grated Cheddar cheese
> 1 egg, beaten
> ¼ pint double cream
> Small pinch of sage

Sift the flour with the salt into a bowl. Add the fat, cut into small pieces and, using two knives or a pastry cutter, cut the fat into the flour until the mixture resembles coarse breadcrumbs. Mix in the egg and add enough cold water to make a firm dough. Cover the pastry with a cloth and chill in a refrigerator for 20–30 minutes before rolling out. Divide the pastry in half and roll one half to line a 7-inch flan case.

Peel and finely chop the onion. Melt ¼ oz butter in a small sauce-pan or frying pan, add the onion and cook over a low heat, stirring continually, until the onion is soft and transparent.

Peel, core and thinly slice the apples. Arrange half the apples in a layer on the bottom of the flan, cover with the onions, sprinkle over half the sugar, salt, pepper and a very small pinch of sage and half the cheese. Repeat the layers with the remaining ingredients. Dampen the edges of the pastry and cover with the remaining pastry rolled out thinly. Pinch the edges tightly together, flute them neatly with the back of a fork and brush over with beaten egg. Cut two vents in the top and bake in a hot oven (400° F. Reg. 6) for 30 minutes until the pastry is crisp and golden brown. Leave to cool for 2 minutes.

Heat the cream without boiling and pour it carefully through a funnel through one of the air vents.

Devonshire Sausage and Apple Cakes

Serves 4

½ lb lean pork
½ lb fat belly pork
1 small onion
1 oz fresh white breadcrumbs
1 teaspoon fresh finely chopped sage or pinch
dried sage
Salt and freshly ground black pepper
3 cooking apples
Flour
2 oz butter
2 oz lard

Soak the breadcrumbs in 3 tablespoons water for 30 minutes. Squeeze out excess water. Put the lean and fat pork followed by the breadcrumbs through the fine blades of a mincer. Repeat the process to ensure that the meat is finely minced. Finely chop the onion. Combine the pork, breadcrumbs and onion in a basin, mix in the sage and season generously with salt and pepper. Shape the mixture into eight cakes.

Peel the apples, remove the core and cut apples into thin rings. Dip each slice in the flour and fry until golden in ½ oz butter mixed with ½ oz lard, drain on kitchen paper and keep warm on a serving dish.

Fry the pork cakes in the remaining butter and lard until they are crisp and golden brown on both sides. Arrange the cakes on the fried apple rings and serve at once with mashed potatoes.

Bubble and Squeak

So called because the sound of squeaking which comes from the frying cabbage and potatoes is supposed to represent the sounds of witches trying to escape from the heat of the fire. To my mind, this is such a delicious and economical dish that it is well worth cooking extra quantities of mashed potatoes and cabbage whenever they are to be served as a plain accompaniment to a main course.

Serves 4

1½ oz dripping or bacon fat
2 rashers streaky bacon
1 onion
1 small cabbage
1½ lb potatoes
Salt and freshly ground black pepper
1 tablespoon finely chopped parsley

Peel the potatoes and cook them in boiling salted water until soft. Drain well and mash until smooth. Finely shred the cabbage and cook it in boiling salted water for 10 minutes and drain well. Mix the cabbage with the mashed potato and season with salt and freshly ground black pepper. Remove the rinds from the bacon and finely chop the rashers. Peel and finely chop the onion.

Heat the dripping or bacon fat in a heavy frying pan. Add the bacon and onion and cook over a low heat until the onion is soft and transparent. Mix in the potatoes and cabbage and press down firmly to cover the pan in an even layer. Fry over a high heat for 10 minutes until the underneath is a crisp golden brown. Invert on to a heated serving dish and top with finely chopped parsley. *Note:* Served with four fried eggs on top of it, Bubble and Squeak makes an excellent supper dish.

Frugal Finney

I think it is fair to say that courgettes have now taken over from the watery, rather tasteless marrow in most parts of the country. They grow well in warmer gardens, are madly prolific and have a good texture and flavour which adds a lot to our basic range of vegetables. This recipe is another of those vegetable dishes which can stand on its own as a main course.

Serves 4

1½ lb courgettes
2½ oz butter
4 spring onions
1 lb tomatoes
Salt and freshly ground black pepper
2 tablespoons flour
¾ pint milk
2 oz Cheddar cheese, grated
3 tablespoons brown breadcrumbs

Chop the onions and peel and slice the tomatoes. Cut the courgettes into ½-inch thick slices. Melt 1½ oz butter in a frying pan, add the onion and cook over a low heat until the onion is soft and transparent. Add the tomatoes and cook for a further 5 minutes. Arrange the courgettes, onion and tomato in layers in a baking dish. Season each layer with salt and pepper and pour over the juices from the pan. Cover with tinfoil and cook for 20 minutes in a moderately hot oven (375° F. Reg. 5).

Melt 1 oz butter in a saucepan, add the flour and mix well. Gradually blend in the milk, stirring continuously over a medium high heat until the sauce is thick and smooth. Drain off the juice from the courgette mixture, add it to the sauce and season with salt and pepper as necessary.

Place the courgette mixture in a clean fireproof dish, pour over the sauce and top with the combined crumbs and grated cheese. Cook under a hot grill until the top is golden brown and bubbling.

Pan Haggerty

A dish that seems to crop up in many parts of the country in one guise or another.

Serves 6

2 lb potatoes
1 lb onions
1 tablespoon dripping
3 oz grated Cheddar cheese
Salt and freshly ground black pepper
1 tablespoon finely chopped parsley

Peel and thinly slice the potatoes and the onions.

Melt the dripping in a heavy frying pan. Cover the bottom of the pan with a layer of potatoes, followed by a thin layer of onions and some of the grated cheese and season with salt and pepper. Continue the layers until all the ingredients are used up.

Place over a medium heat, cover with a saucepan lid or tinfoil and cook for about 30 minutes until the bottom is well browned and the vegetables are cooked through. Invert on to a heated serving dish, sprinkle with finely chopped parsley and serve at once.

Purée of Spinach or Sorrel with Onions and Bacon

Serves 4–6

1½ lb fresh spinach or sorrel leaves

2 onions

2 oz butter

1 tablespoon flour

½ teaspoon ground nutmeg

½ teaspoon sugar

Salt and freshly ground black pepper

¼ pint gravy or stock

2 tablespoons double cream

2 rashers bacon

Remove any tough stalks, wash the spinach or sorrel in plenty of cold water, drain well and pat dry on a clean cloth. Peel and finely chop the onions. Melt the butter, add the onions and cook over a low heat until the onion is soft and transparent. Add the spinach or sorrel, stirring until it is wilted. Sprinkle over the flour and mix well. Stir in the stock, add the nutmeg, sugar and seasoning, bring to the boil, cover and simmer for about 15 minutes until tender.

Fry the bacon rashers without extra fat until crisp. Drain on kitchen paper and crumble into small pieces.

Purée the spinach or sorrel through a sieve or food mill and return to a clean pan. Beat in the cream, check the seasoning and serve piping hot with the bacon pieces scattered on top.

7
Sauces and Things

In this chapter are the good old English sauces that have withstood the ravages of time together with some old-fashioned sauces which may have been almost forgotten, but which I feel deserve be resurrected – such things as devilled sauce and caper sauce, a rich love apple (or tomato) sauce which bears no resemblance to that very ordinary substance which comes with such reluctance from the bottle, or a really tart and flavoursome apple sauce.

Also in this section are those recipes which come in no other defined category. Recipes for tea time treats and old-fashioned pickles and the ultimate sophistication of pickled peaches (a recipe I have until now guarded jealously and which I have only ever come across in one other household), which turns a few slices of cold tongue and ham into picnic fare that is indeed 'something else'.

SWEET AND SAVOURY SAUCES

Sauces seem to be as much a question of vogue and fashion as anything else. In the early days they were sharply flavoured with herbs and spices to disguise the flavour of meat or game that might be on the high side. In the eighteenth century they were usually copies of French and continental sauces and in the Victorian era they settled down, as did so many things, into rich blandness. In these days of economic complexity, good sauces can do much to enliven and titivate many basic and mundane dishes.

Make good use of fresh herbs when they are available. Use mushroom ketchup or anchovies as flavouring ingredients and remember that the addition of a little double cream or a beaten egg yolk may sound like an unnecessary extravagance but the lift such little things can give is enormous.

Apple and Mint Sauce

Serve with hot or cold roast lamb or pork.

1 cooking apple
3 tablespoons redcurrant jelly
1 tablespoon white or red wine vinegar

2 tablespoons very finely chopped mint
Salt, pepper and a pinch of cayenne

Heat the jelly in a saucepan until it is runny. Leave to cool but not set. Peel the apple and coarsely grate the flesh. Mix the apple, vinegar, mint and seasoning into the jelly and serve cold.

Brandy Butter

3 oz unsalted butter
3 oz icing sugar
3 tablespoons brandy

Soften the butter. Beat well, gradually adding the icing sugar and continuing to beat until the butter is almost white and very fluffy. Gradually add the brandy, still beating all the time.

Creamy Marmalade Sauce

Delicious with all steamed or baked puddings.

Serves 4

2 tablespoons marmalade
¼ gill double cream

Combine the marmalade and cream in a saucepan and heat over a low flame, stirring continuously until the marmalade has melted – do not allow the sauce to boil. *Note:* A little sherry can be added to the sauce.

Pear and Ginger Sauce

For Ice Cream, Sponge Puddings and Pancakes

Serves 4

2 ripe eating pears
3 oz preserved ginger in syrup
6 oz golden syrup
¼ teaspoon ground ginger

Peel and halve the pears, remove the cores and cut the flesh into small dice. Finely chop the preserved ginger.

Pour the golden syrup into a saucepan, heat until melted and mix in the ground ginger. Add the pear and ginger pieces and cook over a low heat for about 15 minutes until the pear is soft but not pulpy.

Serve hot. *Note:* The sauce can be stored in screw-top jars and used later.

Plum Sauce

Serve plum sauce with roast chicken, duck or lamb.

Anyone who likes the flavour of sharp fruit sauces such as A.1 or O.K. will immediately fall for this tangy, sweet–sour taste. If you make it when plums are well in season, the sauce is extremely inexpensive and it keeps well.

> 2½ lb English cooking plums
> 1 lb onions
> ¼ pint malt vinegar
> 2 teaspoons salt
> 1 teaspoon ground ginger, allspice,
> nutmeg and English mustard powder
> ¼ teaspoon ground cloves
> 4 oz soft brown sugar

Peel and finely chop the onions and combine with all the other ingredients in a large saucepan. Bring to the boil, cover and simmer for 30 minutes. Cool, remove the stones from the plums and purée the mixture through a food mill, a coarse sieve or in an electric liquidizer. Return to a clean pan, bring back to the boil and simmer for 1 hour. Pack into jars while still hot and cover tightly.

Bread Sauce

An excellent accompaniment for roast chicken.

> 1 onion, peeled
> 4 cloves
> ½ pint milk
> 2 oz fresh white breadcrumbs
> ½ teaspoon finely grated lemon rind
> 1 tablespoon double cream
> 1 oz butter
> Salt and white pepper

Stick the cloves into the onion and put it into a saucepan with the milk. Bring to the boil then mix in the breadcrumbs and lemon rind.

Season with salt and pepper, return to the boil and then simmer for 15 minutes. Remove the onion and cloves and mix in the cream and 1 oz butter. Check seasoning before serving.

Caper Sauce

Traditionally this is an accompaniment for mutton but it goes well with boiled fowl and with fish. It has a tart taste that children tend to turn up their noses at, but I find it popular with grown-ups, and also that it makes a good sauce to pep up an uninteresting boiled vegetable.

Makes approx. 1 pint of sauce

> *1 small shallot or 4 spring onions*
> *1 oz butter*
> *1 tablespoon flour*
> *¾ pint white stock*
> *1½ tablespoons capers*
> *1 egg yolk*
> *3 tablespoons double cream*
> *Salt and white pepper*
> *1 tablespoon finely chopped parsley*

Peel and very finely chop the shallot or spring onions. Chop the capers. Melt ½ oz butter in a heavy saucepan. Add the chopped shallot or onions and cook over a low heat until soft. Add the flour and mix well. Gradually blend in the stock, stirring continually over a medium heat until the sauce comes to the boil and is thick and smooth. Add the capers and simmer for 2 minutes. Beat the egg yolk with the cream, add this to the sauce and mix thoroughly but do not allow to boil. Blend in the remaining ½ oz butter and the parsley and season with salt and pepper. *Note:* Try serving this sauce with Poor Man's Asparagus (see page 118).

Chicken Giblet Sauce

The sauce can be served with any roast poultry.

Admittedly this sauce is a bore to make but so are many of the best dishes in the world. If, like me, you look upon cooking as a relaxing therapy then recipes like this are almost a joy to produce.

The giblets of 1 chicken
½ pint stock
¼ oz chicken dripping or butter
1 small onion
Bouquet garni
1 slice white bread with the crusts removed
1 tablespoon cider vinegar
Salt and freshly ground black pepper
2 tablespoons red wine or port

Finely chop the onion and combine it with the chicken neck, heart, gizzard, bouquet garni and stock. Bring to the boil and simmer slowly for 30 minutes. Strain off the stock.

Cook the chicken liver in the chicken fat or butter for 3 minutes, mince it with the bread through the fine blades of a mincing machine and return it to a clean pan with the strained stock. Add the red wine or port, season with salt and pepper and add the cider vinegar to sharpen the sauce. Cook for 3 minutes and adjust seasoning as necessary.

A Sauce for Roast Chicken

This sauce, which makes excellent use of the giblets from a chicken, is one that I cannot speak too highly of. It will pep up the taste of a roast chicken in the most amazing way and has been so successful at Maidenwell that a venerable gentleman eating at my table once got so excited about it that he forgot about his succulent chicken thigh and made a meal of the sauce alone.

Makes approx. ¾ pint of stock

The heart, gizzard, liver and neck of
one chicken (preferably 2 if possible)
1 small onion
1 oz butter
¼ pint port
½ pint stock
Salt and freshly ground black pepper
Pinch mixed herbs or a bouquet garni

Finely chop the gizzard, heart and liver. Peel and finely chop the onion. Melt the butter in a saucepan, add the onion, the chopped giblets and the neck and cook over a high heat to brown the meat, stirring to prevent sticking or burning. Add the port, stock and herbs, season with salt and freshly ground black pepper, bring to the boil and simmer for 30 minutes until the gizzard is tender.

Remove from the stove, take out the bouquet garni and the neck. Pick off all the meat you can from the neck, chop it finely and return it to the sauce. Thin the sauce with a little more stock if necessary and check the seasoning before serving.

Cumberland Sauce

For cold ham, tongue, duck or venison.

> Juice and peel of 1 orange
> Juice and peel of $\frac{1}{2}$ lemon
> 4 tablespoons redcurrant jelly
> 1 shallot or very small onion
> $\frac{1}{4}$ pint port
> 1 teaspoon made English mustard
> $\frac{1}{8}$ teaspoon ground ginger
> Salt and freshly ground black pepper

Very thinly pare the rind from the orange and lemon making sure that no white membrane remains on the skin. Blanch the rind in boiling water for 3 minutes and drain well.

Peel and very finely chop the shallot. Combine the shallot and redcurrant jelly in a saucepan and cook over a low heat, stirring every now and then until the jelly has melted. Combine the mustard and ginger and gradually mix in the orange and lemon juice. Add the juices to the redcurrant jelly with the port and peel, bring to the boil, season with a little salt and pepper and simmer for 10 minutes. Serve hot or cold.

Gooseberry Sauce

For fish or roast duck.

Those who collect cookery books with traditional recipes may be rather bored with this classic sauce. I found a recipe that recommended using the red, rather than the green variety of gooseberries, and the sauce that evolved was so delicious I have frozen vast quantities of it and serve it with anything from fried fish to plain roast chicken. The sauce has a pleasant pinkish tinge.

Makes approx. ¾ pint sauce – enough for 4 servings

1½ oz butter
1 small onion
½ lb red gooseberries
2 tablespoons stock
½ teaspoon dry mustard
2 tablespoons dry white wine
2 tablespoons caster sugar
Salt and freshly ground black pepper

Peel and very finely chop the onion. Top and tail the gooseberries. Heat 1 oz butter, add the onion and cook over a low heat until the onion is soft and transparent. Add the mustard and mix well.

Add the gooseberries, stock, white wine, sugar and seasoning, bring to the boil, cover and simmer for 20 minutes until the gooseberries are soft. Purée the gooseberries through a fine sieve, a food mill or in an electrical liquidizer and return to a clean pan.

Blend in the remaining ½ oz butter, heat through and check seasoning before serving. Serve with grilled mackerel, roast duck or chicken and any other plainly cooked food that needs a 'lift'.

Hot Devil Sauce

Serve with cold meats or cover cold slices of ham with the mixture and put under the grill for a few minutes to make an excellent supper dish.

1 teaspoon Branston or other pickle
1 teaspoon made English mustard
1 teaspoon anchovy essence
1 teaspoon red or white wine vinegar
1 teaspoon honey
½ teaspoon fruit sauce (A.1 or Daddies
sauce will do as well)
½ teaspoon Worcestershire sauce
¼ pint double cream
Salt

Combine the pickle with the mustard, anchovy essence, vinegar, honey, fruit sauce and Worcestershire sauce and mix well. Whip the cream until thick and fold it into the other ingredients. Season with a little salt if necessary.

Love Apple Sauce

Did you know that common, everyday tomatoes used to go by the name of 'love apples'? This is a traditional 'love apple' sauce and, although it tastes the same as a tomato sauce, no one, I'm sure, will deny that the old name has an edge over just plain 'tomato'. As one of the classic, basic ingredient sauces, this can be used as a dressing for hot vegetables, a sauce for macaroni or other pasta, with made-up fish or meat dishes or as a base for nourishing soups.

> 1 lb ripe tomatoes
> 3 shallots
> Sprig thyme
> 2 sage leaves, finely chopped
> 1 tablespoon finely chopped parsley
> 2 cloves garlic
> 3 tablespoons olive oil
> 1 teaspoon sugar
> Salt and freshly ground black pepper
> 1 teaspoon white wine vinegar
> ½ oz butter

Roughly chop the tomatoes. Peel and finely chop the shallots. Peel and very finely chop the garlic. Heat the oil, add the shallots and garlic and cook over a low heat until the onion is soft and transparent. Add the tomatoes, herbs and sugar. Then season with salt and freshly ground black pepper and stir in the vinegar. Bring to the boil, cover tightly and simmer for 30 minutes. Rub through a fine sieve, or process through a food mill. Return to a clean pan, add the butter and check seasoning before serving.

Mayonnaise

Napoleon's chef is supposed to have invented this marvellous cold food sauce at the time of the battle of Mahon. Whether this is fact or fiction, mayonnaise had become popular in England by the time of the mid-nineteenth century. Since then we seem to have forgotten one or two ingredients that were an essential part of the classic sauce. A little water added to the mayonnaise at the last minute gives it that lovely pale look and dispels any cloying taste that may be present in the olive oil used for the recipe. A little cayenne pepper added to the ingredients which make up the base of the sauce gives it a slightly piquant flavouring that I find delicious. Mayonnaise should never be too bland and the basic recipe can be varied in a number of exciting ways to complement a wide variety of dishes. The following is a Victorian interpretation of a traditional mayonnaise.

> 2 egg yolks
> Salt and white pepper
> ⅓ teaspoon cayenne pepper
> ¼ teaspoon made English mustard
> 1½ gills good olive oil
> 3 tablespoons white wine vinegar
> 1 tablespoon cold water

Beat the egg yolks with a little salt and pepper, the cayenne and mustard until smooth and very well blended. Add the oil, a teaspoon at a time, beating strongly with a wooden spoon until each addition of oil has been incorporated and the mixture emulsifies. When all the oil has been used, beat in the vinegar a little at a time and finally blend in the water. Check the seasoning before serving. *Note:* I know people who short cut the making of mayonnaise by using an electric liquidizer or mixer. I don't have many old-fashioned ideas but I do feel there is all the difference in the world between the taste of mayonnaise made by hard graft and a lot of hand beating and one made in a machine.

Sorrel Mayonnaise

If you can lay your hands on some fresh sorrel, this variation of a basic mayonnaise makes a delicious accompaniment to cold poached or baked salmon or sea trout.

> Basic mayonnaise (see page 161)
> 12 leaves sorrel

Wash the sorrel leaves and plunge them into boiling, salted water. Boil for 5 minutes until soft, drain well and pat dry with a clean towel. Purée the leaves through a fine sieve or food mill, leave to cool and then blend the purée with the mayonnaise. Check seasoning before serving. *Note:* I am never very keen on using artificial aids in cooking but I find with this sauce a sparing drop of green vegetable colouring gives it a more attractive appearance.

Stilton Mayonnaise

This makes an unusual sauce that goes well with grilled or fried fish.

>Basic mayonnaise (see page 161)
>2 oz Stilton cheese
>A little cayenne pepper

Mash the cheese with a fork. Add 2 tablespoons mayonnaise and beat until smooth. Gradually blend in the remaining mayonnaise and season with a little cayenne pepper.

Old English Egg and Mustard Sauce

Serve with fish or vegetables.

>1 hard-boiled egg
>1 oz butter
>2 tablespoons flour
>½ pint milk
>2 teaspoons English mustard powder
>2 teaspoons vinegar
>2 tablespoons double cream
>Salt and pepper

Finely chop the egg. Melt the butter, add the flour and mix well. Gradually blend in the milk, stirring continually over a medium high heat until the sauce comes to the boil and is thick and smooth. Mix the mustard to a paste with the vinegar, add to the sauce, mix well and simmer for 3 minutes. Stir in the cream and chopped egg and season with salt and pepper.

Parsley Sauce

A richer flavour is given to this simple but pleasant sauce by mincing rather than chopping the parsley. Serve it with fish or chicken.

>1½ oz butter
>2½ tablespoons flour
>¼ pint milk
>¼ pint chicken stock
>¼ pint single cream
>1 small bunch parsley

2 teaspoons lemon juice
Salt, pepper and pinch nutmeg

Melt the butter, add the flour and mix well over a medium heat. Gradually add the milk and stock, stirring continually, until the sauce comes to the boil and is thick and smooth. Remove from the heat.

Remove the stalks of the parsley sprigs and mince or very finely chop the leaves. Add the parsley to the sauce, return to a low heat, season with salt, pepper and a pinch of nutmeg and blend in the lemon juice. Cook gently for 3 minutes, add cream and mix well but do not boil.

SWEET AND SAVOURY THINGS

All-year-round Fruit Salad

For this ever-ready pudding you need two large glass jars with screw-top lids (large sweet jars from a confectioner would be ideal).

Fresh fruit
Sugar
Rum

Slice fresh fruit as it is in season and place it in layers in the jars. Cover each layer with sugar, more or less according to the sweetness of the fruit, and with 1 tablespoon of rum to each layer of fruit. Screw the jar tightly after each addition and keep in a cool, dark place. The salad is ready a year from the time when the first fruit was put into the jars.

Candied Plums

A delicious sweetmeat to make when plums are cheap and plentiful. Choose ripe eating plums that are firm and unblemished.

Serves 4

1 . lb plums
1 lb sugar
½ pint water

Wipe the plums, cut a slit in the side of each one and carefully remove the stone. Combine the sugar and water, bring to the boil and continue boiling until the syrup will drop in beads from a spoon.

Drop the plums into the syrup and simmer over a low heat until the plums are transparent. Lift them out with a slotted spoon and place on a piece of marble or on a lightly oiled baking sheet to dry. Leave for 24 hours then reheat the syrup, put in the plums and cook them for a further 20 minutes. Lift out, place on greaseproof paper and bake in a very low oven (200° F. Reg. ½) until crisp and dry. These can be served chilled with whipped cream as a sweet course.

Parkin

Parkin is traditionally served on Bonfire Night. It should be made two weeks in advance and kept in a sealed tin to mature. If, like me, you like a drop of the 'hard stuff', I can highly recommend pricking the parkin lightly with a fork and sprinkling it with a little rum before sealing it.

> 6 oz plain flour
> 1 teaspoon salt
> 1 teaspoon ground ginger
> 1½ teaspoons cinnamon
> 1 teaspoon bicarbonate of soda
> 10 oz rolled oats
> 4 fluid oz black treacle
> 2 fluid oz golden syrup
> 5 oz butter
> 4 oz soft brown sugar
> ¼ pint milk
> 1 egg

Sift together the flour, salt, spices and bicarbonate of soda. Add the oats and mix well.

Combine the treacle, syrup, butter and milk and sugar in a saucepan and heat gently until the butter has melted. Cool, add the egg and beat with a wire whisk to make sure all the ingredients are well blended.

Make a well in the centre of the dry ingredients. Pour in the liquids and beat with a wooden spoon until smooth.

Line a 7-inch square baking tin with lightly oiled greaseproof paper, pour in the mixture and cook in the centre of a moderately hot oven (350° F. Reg. 4) for 50–60 minutes, until a skewer plunged into the centre of the parkin will come out clean. If the top of the parkin shows any sign of browning, cover it with a sheet of dampened greaseproof paper.

Welsh Cakes

½ lb self-raising flour
4 oz lard
4 oz currants
¼ teaspoon salt
2 oz sugar
1 small egg
¼ pint milk

Rub the lard into the flour until the mixture resembles coarse breadcrumbs. Mix in the currants, salt and sugar. Lightly beat the egg with the milk, add to the dry ingredients and mix with a fork. Knead the mixture lightly to form a smooth dough. Roll out on a floured board to ¼ inch thickness and cut into circles with a floured pastry cutter.

Rub a heavy frying pan or griddle with a little lard. Cook the cakes for 5 minutes on each side until they are firm and golden brown. Keep the cakes warm in a napkin and serve with butter and jam.

Salted Almonds

A far cheaper way of having salted almonds than buying them from a shop. They can also be served on the dinner table as an accompaniment to soup.

½ lb blanched almonds
1½ oz butter
½ tablespoon olive oil
Salt

Combine the butter and oil in a frying pan and heat until foaming. Add the almonds and cook over a moderately high heat, shaking the pan until the almonds are a rich golden colour.

Put a generous amount of salt in a paper bag, add the almonds while they are still hot and shake the bag until the almonds are well coated with salt. Spread on to kitchen paper and leave to cool.

Devilled Salted Almonds

Add $\frac{1}{4}$ teaspoon cayenne pepper to the butter in the pan and continue as above.

Curried Almonds

Add $\frac{1}{4}$ teaspoon curry powder to the butter and continue as above.

Brown Bread and Cucumber Sandwiches

Cucumber sandwiches are evocative of everything that is British, but they have to be properly made. It is no good slapping together slabs of bread with the crusts left on, stuffed with thick slices of unpeeled cucumber, and hoping that they will evoke memories of hot summers, smooth lawns, the click of croquet balls and brass bands by the village cricket pitch. Like all the best things in life, cucumber sandwiches should be perfect.

Wafer thin slices of thinly buttered brown
bread with the crusts removed
Cucumber
Salt
White wine vinegar
White pepper

Peel and very, very thinly slice the cucumber. Place it in a dish, pour over a little vinegar, sprinkle generously with salt and leave to stand for 30 minutes. Drain well.

Spread the buttered bread with a layer of cucumber slices, sprinkle with a little pepper and sandwich together neatly. Press firmly and cut into neat fingers about 2 inches wide. Wrap the sandwiches in a slightly dampened white damask napkin.

Curried Egg Sandwiches

Thin slices of white bread with the crusts removed
2 hard-boiled eggs
1½ oz softened butter
1 teaspoon curry powder

Chop the eggs and then mash them with the butter and curry powder. Spread on the bread, sandwich neatly and cut into 2-inch fingers.

Tomato and Cheese Toasts

Serves 4

4 slices thick cut white bread
1 lb tomatoes
1 oz butter
1 tablespoon sugar
Salt and freshly ground black pepper
2 oz Cheddar cheese
Made English mustard

Peel the tomatoes by plunging in boiling water for a few minutes and then peeling off the skin. Cut into thin slices, and combine them with the butter, sugar and some salt and freshly ground black pepper in a saucepan. Cook over a low heat, stirring occasionally until the mixture comes to the boil. Cover and simmer for 10 minutes.

Toast the bread and remove the crusts. Cut the cheese into very thin slices. Spread the toast with the tomato mixture and cover with the thin slices of cheese. Spread the cheese lightly with mustard and grill under a medium high heat until the cheese is golden brown and bubbling. Serve at once.

Anchovy Rarebits

Serves 4

1 oz butter
6 oz grated Cheedar cheese
2 egg yolks
2 teaspoons anchovy essence
½ teaspoon made English mustard
½ tablespoon white wine vinegar
Salt and a pinch paprika
4 slices toast with the crusts removed

Beat the egg yolks until smooth. Melt the butter, add the egg yolks, cheese, anchovy essence, mustard and vinegar and cook over a low heat, stirring gently, until the mixture is the consistency of creamy scrambled eggs. Season with salt and paprika, spoon over the toast and serve at once.

Canapés Indiennes

Many of the late nineteenth- and early twentieth-century popular dishes had an East Indian background with overtones of curry and hot spices. With the Edwardians this frequently took the guise of savouries. Now that the days of silver salvers and butlers are merely nostalgic yearnings for most of us, these delicious savoury recipes make excellent lunch or light supper dishes.

Serves 2 as a main course or 4 as a savoury

> 4 slices white bread
> 2 oz lard
> 1½ oz butter
> 3 shallots
> 2 tablespoons curry powder
> 1 tablespoon cream
> 1 tablespoon milk
> 2 tablespoons mango chutney, finely chopped
> 6 oz poached smoked haddock

Remove the crusts from the bread and cut each slice into four fingers. Heat the lard until smoking, add the bread fingers and cook until golden brown on both sides. Drain on kitchen paper and keep warm.

Peel and finely chop the shallots and flake the haddock with a fork. Melt half the butter in a saucepan, add the shallots and cook over a low heat until the shallots are soft and transparent. Add the curry powder and mango chutney, mix well and gradually blend in the milk and cream, stirring continually. Do not boil. Cook over a very slow heat for 10 minutes. Melt the remaining butter in another saucepan, add the smoked haddock and heat through. Spread the haddock on the fried bread fingers, pour over the curry sauce and brown quickly under a hot grill. Serve at once.

Devilled Sardine Puffs

Serves 4

4 oz puff pastry
1 anchovy fillet
⅛ teaspoon English mustard powder
Pinch cayenne pepper
Salt and pepper
8 sardines
1 small egg, beaten

Drain oil from sardines and anchovy fillet. Pat sardines dry with kitchen paper. Combine mustard, cayenne pepper and anchovy in a mortar and pound smooth with a pestle.

Roll pastry out thinly. Divide into eight pieces about 3 inches wide and as long as the sardines. Place a sardine in the centre of each oblong of pastry, spread each sardine with some of the paste, and roll up neatly like sausage rolls. Brush rolls with beaten egg seasoned with a little salt and pepper and bake in a hot oven (425° F. Reg. 7) for 15–20 minutes until puffed and golden brown.

Herring Roe Savoury

Serves 4

4 slices bread
Lard for frying
6 herring roes
2 oz flour
1 white of egg
½ gill warm water
¼ tablespoon olive or vegetable oil
4 thin rashers streaky bacon
2 tomatoes

Remove the crusts from the bread and cut each slice in half. Fry the bread in the lard until golden brown on both sides. Thinly slice the tomatoes, arrange them on a lightly greased baking sheet, sprinkle with salt and freshly ground black pepper and bake in a moderate oven (350° F. Reg. 4) for about 5 minutes. Fry bacon, without extra fat, until crisp.

To make the batter combine flour and water and beat until

smooth. Whip egg white until stiff and fold into the batter mixture. Wash roes, cut each one in half and pat dry on kitchen paper. Dip them in batter and fry until golden crisp in smoking hot, deep olive or vegetable oil.

Cover the fried bread with sliced tomato, top each piece with half a bacon rasher and pieces of fried roe. Heat through quickly in a hot oven and serve at once.

Potted Lobster

8 oz cooked lobster
3 oz butter
Salt and white pepper
Pinch mace, nutmeg and ground cloves

Heat the butter until foaming but not brown. Add the lobster, spices and seasoning and cook for 2 minutes. Remove half the lobster pieces and pound the remaining lobster with the butter to a smooth paste (this can be done in a pestle with a mortar, through a food mill or in an electric liquidizer). Mix in the reserved lobster pieces, check the seasoning and pack in an earthenware jar or terrine. Serve as a first course with hot toast and quarters of lemon or as a filling for very special sandwiches.

Scotch Woodcock

I once included Scotch woodcock in one of my cookery articles for the *Sunday Telegraph* and received a flurry of letters as a result. There are, I discovered, far more ways than one to prepare this excellent savoury and those who enjoy it take the matter extremely seriously.

The following recipe is one that I came across in a Victorian cookery book. It gives yet another slant to the dish and though rich it is, to my mind, the best interpretation I have yet discovered.

Serves 4

4 slices white bread
Butter
8 fillets anchovies

2 egg yolks
½ pint double cream
Salt and white pepper

Finely chop the anchovy fillets. Beat the egg yolks with the cream. Toast the bread, remove the crusts and butter each slice. Spread two slices of toast with the chopped anchovy fillets and make two sandwiches. Cut each toasted sandwich into three fingers and keep warm while making the topping.

Cook the egg yolks and cream in a non-stick pan, over a low heat, stirring constantly until they are the consistency of lightly scrambled egg – do not overcook. Season with salt and pepper and pour over the toast fingers. Serve at once.

Beef Marrow on Toast

This has the dual role of providing both a sensational accompaniment to soups and a rich stock. A butcher will usually let you have marrow bones free or for a small cost.

Serves 4

4 beef marrow bones
2 large onions
2 carrots
2 tomatoes
1 stick celery with leaves
Salt and pepper
8 peppercorns
2 bay leaves
2 sprigs parsley
1 sprig thyme
2 sage leaves
4 slices toast

Wipe onions with a damp cloth but leave the skins on and cut into quarters. Halve tomatoes. Wash and roughly chop carrots. Roughly chop celery sticks and leaves. Tie herbs in a small piece of muslin.

Roast marrow bones in a hot oven (425° F. Reg. 7) for 15 minutes until beginning to brown. Cool and wrap the cut ends in tinfoil. Place bones and any juices from the roasting pan in a saucepan with the vegetables, herbs and seasoning. Cover with cold water, bring to the boil, cover and simmer for 2 hours.

Remove the bones from the stock, leave until cool enough to handle and scoop out the marrow with a marrow or pickle spoon. Mash the marrow, season with salt and pepper and spread on hot toast.

To make a rich stock, return the bones to the pan with any other available bones or poultry carcasses and continue to simmer for a further 2 hours. Strain, cool and remove the fat from the surface.

Gammon Sandwich

Serves 4

> 4 gammon rashers
> 4 tomatoes
> 6 oz Cheddar cheese
> Mustard
> Salt and pepper
> ½ oz melted butter

Remove the rind from the gammon, brush the rashers with melted butter and grill under a medium heat for about 10 minutes or until gammon is cooked through. Arrange the slices in a fireproof serving dish. Spread a little mustard on each one.

Thinly slice the tomatoes and cheese. Top the gammon rashers with tomato slices, season with salt and pepper and cover with the cheese. Cook for a further 3 minutes under a hot grill until the cheese has melted and is golden and bubbly.

Hunter's Sandwich

Invented for the hungry shooter, this makes a good picnic dish. The sandwich used to be made in a sandwich loaf, but as that resulted in a large proportion of crumb to meat I prefer to make it in a French loaf.

> 1 French loaf
> 1 lb rump steak
> Olive oil
> ¼ lb mushrooms
> 1½ oz butter
> Salt and freshly ground black pepper
> A little English mustard

Brush the steak with a little olive oil and grill under a hot flame to medium rare. Cut into thin strips. Very thinly slice the mushrooms and fry them for 3 minutes in the butter. Season well with salt and freshly ground black pepper.

Cut the loaf in half lengthways and remove most of the soft crumb. Place the steak on the bottom half, spread with a little mustard, cover with the mushrooms and the juices from the pan and replace the top of the loaf. Wrap tightly in tinfoil and press down with a weighted board. Refrigerate for 4 hours before cutting into thick slices.

Petty Patties

Occasionally one comes across sweetbreads on the menu of a restaurant, but I don't think I have ever eaten them in any private house other than my own. I have never discovered why. Sweetbreads are, to my mind, a most delicious, inexpensive and nourishing form of food. Their slight blandness lends itself to a large variety of recipes of which this traditional, beautifully named dish is one of the best.

Serves 6

Pastry
8 oz plain flour
4 oz butter
¼ teaspoon salt
1 small egg
Cold water

Filling
1 lb sweetbreads
1 egg, beaten
Dried breadcrumbs
Oil for frying
1 onion
2 oz butter
1½ tablespoons flour
½ pint milk
1 teaspoon French Dijon mustard
2 oz ham, finely chopped
1 tablespoon finely chopped parsley

Salt and freshly ground black pepper
1 tablespoon dry sherry

To make the pastry combine the flour and salt in a bowl. Cut the butter into small pieces and then, using two sharp knives, cut the fat into the flour until the mixture resembles coarse breadcrumbs. Make a well in the centre and break in the egg. Gradually incorporate the egg into the flour, pulling the flour into the egg with your hands. When the egg is mixed with the flour, add enough ice-cold water to make a stiffish dough. Wrap the pastry in a floured cloth and chill in a refrigerator for 30 minutes before rolling out.

Roll the pastry out thinly and line twelve 6-inch diameter patty moulds or twenty-four tartlet moulds. Fill the centre of the un-cooked pastry with dried beans or peas and bake 'blind' in a hot oven (425° F. Reg. 7) for 10 minutes, then lower the temperature to moderate (350° F. Reg. 4) and continue to cook for a further 10–15 minutes until the pastry is a light golden brown. Remove the beans and leave to cool.

Soak the sweetbreads in cold water for 30 minutes. Drain well, pat dry on kitchen paper and carefully trim off any fat or tough membrane. Cut the sweetbreads into slices about ½-inch thick, dip in beaten egg, seasoned with salt and pepper, and then roll in dried breadcrumbs. Heat ½-inch cooking oil in a frying pan, add the sweetbreads and cook over a high heat for about 5 minutes until the sweetbreads are golden brown and cooked through. Drain on kitchen paper.

Peel and finely chop the onion. Melt the butter in a saucepan, add the onion and cook over a low heat until the onion is soft and transparent. Add the flour, mix well and gradually blend in the milk stirring continuously over a medium heat until the sauce is thick and smooth. Bring to the boil and simmer for 3 minutes. Add the mustard, parsley and ham, season with salt and pepper and blend in the sherry. Fold in the fried sweetbreads and leave to cool. Fill the patty cases with the sweetbread mixture, cover lightly with tin-foil and place in a moderate oven (350° F. Reg. 4) for 20 minutes or until hot through.

Potted Shin Beef

A good ingredient for point-to-points, football or spring picnics.

Serves 4

1 lb shin beef
5 oz streaky bacon
Salt, pepper and pinch of nutmeg
Bouquet garni
Bay leaf
Clear stock

Cut the meat into very, very thin slices. Remove the rinds of the bacon and chop the flesh. Arrange alternate layers of meat and bacon in an earthenware dish, sprinkling each layer with salt, pepper and nutmeg. Add the bouquet garni and bay leaf and lay the bacon rinds on top. Pour in just enough stock to cover, cover very tightly and cook in a slow oven (300° F. Reg. 2) for 3 hours or until the meat is fork tender. Remove bacon rinds, bouquet garni and bay leaf, leave to cool and then refrigerate until the juice has set to a clear jelly. Serve with French bread.

Savoury Bacon Potato Cakes

Serves 4

1 lb potatoes (peeled weight)
2 teaspoons salt
Freshly ground black pepper
2 oz butter
3 oz flour
2 oz bacon rashers with the rinds removed

Cook the potatoes in boiling salted water until tender. Drain well and mash until smooth with the seasoning and butter. Finely chop the bacon and fry over a medium heat, without extra fat, for 5 minutes. Drain off excess fat. Beat the flour into the potato mixture and add the bacon pieces. Cool and then roll out to $\frac{1}{4}$-inch thickness on a well floured board. Cut into circles with a floured pastry cutter.

Heat a little bacon fat or lard in a heavy frying pan or a griddle, add the cakes and cook for about 2 minutes on each side until the cakes are golden brown. Serve as quickly as possible.

These cakes go well with soup and I have had a great success by making them about 2 inches in diameter and serving them with the soup course at a dinner party.

8
Puddings and Sweets

Introduced to an Indonesian lady while travelling in the Near East, I was described by my host as 'an English cookery writer' and received with the comment 'Oh, you are a pudding maker then'. So far had the fame of English cooking spread, it seemed, but no further. That lady, at least, was convinced the British survive on 'puddings' alone.

Most of those beloved, nursery-type puddings our menfolk (mine anyway) believe they hunger for came from the Victorian era when having a rich and often extremely heavy pudding as an end to a meal was deemed essential. Earlier the preference was for simpler desserts, light and subtle: rose-flavoured jellies, fruit compotes, syllabubs and creams. Fortunately, cream is still relatively inexpensive if you consider its richness and the expense of producing it, and it is still possible to produce the earlier creations as well as those later bread and butter delights.

Our soft fruits, apples and pears make perfect basic ingredients for a wide range of delicious recipes and the old-fashioned habit of adding a pinch of cinnamon, ginger or nutmeg to fruit pies and tarts is well worth following, although the spices should, of course, be carefully controlled.

FRUIT AND CREAM SWEETS

Pancakes

Pancakes should be very thin and fine. They can be made in advance or frozen; they re-heat well and altogether are the most amenable of puddings.

Serves 4 (2 pancakes each)
> 4 oz plain flour
> Pinch salt
> 1 egg
> 1 oz melted butter
> ½ pint milk
> 2 tablespoons water
> Olive oil
> Juice 1 lemon
> Caster sugar

Sift the flour with the salt into a bowl. Make a well in the centre and add the egg. Gradually beat in the milk and water, working from the centre of the bowl outwards. When all the liquid has been added, pour in the melted butter and beat well with a rotary whisk or electric beater. Brush an omelette pan with a little olive oil. Pour in a tablespoon of batter, swirl it round the pan and pour off any excess as the batter should only just cover the bottom of the pan. Cook over a high heat for about 2 minutes until golden brown on the bottom. Turn the pancake over and cook the other side. Stack cooked pancakes and keep warm.

Pour a little lemon juice over each pancake, sprinkle with sugar and roll up neatly.

For more substantial pancakes fill them with blackberries and sweetened whipped cream just before serving, or try a simple filling of sweet apple sauce. Fine-shred marmalade melted over a low heat makes a tangy filling. The following recipe is reminiscent of a succulent Greek dessert: combine 8 tablespoons of honey, 1 oz of butter, 3 tablespoons of roughly chopped walnuts and the juice of 1 lemon in a saucepan. Cook until hot through and the honey quite liquid. Pour a little of the sauce over each pancake, roll up and serve at once.

Rhubarb Fingers

The combination of fruit and fried bread is a delicious one which seems to have gone out of fashion about fifty years ago. This recipe is something really special and makes a good dinner party climax. It may sound mundane but it certainly doesn't taste it.

Serves 4–6 (about 10 fingers)

> *4 large sticks rhubarb*
> *Slices thick cut white bread*
> *Caster sugar*
> *Butter*
> *1 egg white*
> *1 tablespoon rum*
> *1½ gills double cream*

Trim off the leaves of the rhubarb and any tough strings from the sides. Cut the sticks into 6-inch lengths and steam them in a colander or steamer over a saucepan filled with ¾ pint water. Steam the rhubarb until it is still firm but just tender and leave to cool. Reserve the juice from the steaming.

Remove crusts from bread slices and cut the bread into the same amount of fingers as there are rhubarb lengths, making each one 2 inches wide and 7 inches long. Fry the bread in butter until crisp and lightly golden brown. Drain well on kitchen paper, dredge in caster sugar and leave to cool.

Brush the cold rhubarb sticks with white of egg and roll in caster sugar until coated on all sides. Add enough sugar to the rhubarb juice to sweeten it, bring the liquid to the boil and boil over a high heat until it has reduced and thickened. Add the rum and keep hot.

Beat the cream until thick and spread a good layer on the slices of fried bread. Top each finger with a piece of rhubarb and serve with the sauce passed round separately.

Apple Brown Betty

Serves 4–5

6 oz fresh white breadcrumbs
3 oz unsalted butter
1¾ lb cooking apples (5 large apples)
6 tablespoons golden syrup
Juice 1 lemon
¼ teaspoon cinnamon
2 tablespoons brown sugar

Melt the butter in a heavy frying pan, add the breadcrumbs and cook over a moderately high heat, shaking the pan every now and then to prevent burning, until the crumbs are pale gold in colour.

Peel, core and slice the apples. Combine the syrup, lemon juice and cinnamon in a saucepan and heat through until the syrup has melted. Arrange alternate layers of apples and crumbs in a lightly greased fireproof dish, finishing with a layer of crumbs. Pour over the syrup and lemon juice, sprinkle over the brown sugar, cover with tinfoil and bake in a moderate oven (350° F. Reg. 4) for about 45 minutes until the apples are tender. Remove the tinfoil, raise the heat to hot (400° F. Reg. 6) and cook for a further 10 minutes until the top is crisp and brown. Serve hot or cold with cream.
Note: A delicious Plum Betty can be made the same way. Halve the

plums and remove the stones and sprinkle each layer with a little extra sugar if the plums are very tart.

Apple Humble

Hazelnuts, like blackberries, are common and free. They grow in the hedgerows and if you don't pick them the squirrels will. From October onwards they can also be bought in greengrocers, and the dried varieties are on sale almost all the year round. Cob nuts, the most delicious of all, can also be used for this dish.

Serves 4

> 6 Cox's apples (medium-sized)
> 4 oz granulated sugar
> 2 tablespoons water
> Juice of 1 lemon and grated rind of ½ lemon
> 6 tablespoons rolled oats
> 2 oz butter
> 3 oz hazelnuts

Peel, core and thinly slice the apples and arrange them in a lightly buttered fireproof serving dish. Sprinkle over the sugar and pour over the water mixed with the lemon juice. Finely chop the hazelnuts.

Melt the butter, add the oats, nuts and lemon rind and spread the mixture over the apples. Bake in a moderately hot oven (375° F. Reg. 5) for about 30 minutes until the apple is tender and the topping is golden brown and crisp. Serve hot with cream.

Apple and Rhubarb Charlotte

Serves 4

> ½ pint stewed rhubarb
> ½ pint stewed apples
> Pinch cinnamon
> 2 oz caster sugar
> 2 tablespoons stale sponge cake crumbs
> 2 oz butter
> 6 slices white bread

Lightly grease a solid bottomed 5-inch cake tin. Remove the crusts from the bread. Cut two slices of bread in rounds to cover the bottom of the tin. Melt the butter. Soak all the bread in the butter, line the bottom with one of the rounds, line the side with the rest of the bread, reserving the second round.

Drain off any excess juice from the stewed fruit, mix in the cinnamon, sweeten the fruit with the sugar and stir in the cake crumbs. Pack the fruit into the tin and top with the remaining round of bread. Bake in the centre of a moderately hot oven (350° F. Reg. 4) for 1 hour, covering the top with a piece of greaseproof paper if the bread gets too brown. Turn on to a serving dish and serve hot with cream.

Plum Crumble

Apples, fresh peaches, rhubarb or blackberries can be used instead of plums.

Serves 4

1½ lb cooking plums
2 tablespoons water
3 oz granulated sugar
6 oz plain flour
3 oz butter
3 oz soft brown sugar

Wash the plums, dry them well and remove any stalks. Place plums in a lightly buttered fireproof dish and sprinkle with sugar. Pour over the water.

Mix the flour with the brown sugar and rub in the butter with your fingertips until the mixture resembles fine breadcrumbs. Spread the crumble on the fruit and bake the dish in a hot oven (400° F. Reg. 6) for 10 minutes. Reduce the heat to moderately hot (350° F. Reg. 4) and bake for a further 15 minutes. Serve with cream or custard.

Apricot Chips

Up until the late nineteenth century apricots were grown in profusion in greenhouses all over the country. Now we import them from countries with a hotter climate than our own, with the result that they tend to be sold when on the underripe and rather sharp side. Cut into thin slices and very gently cooked in sugar syrup, these apricot 'chips' keep well and make an attractive

decoration for flans or puddings. They are also delicious mixed
with vanilla ice cream.

Reserve the stones of the apricots and dry them. The kernels
have a marvellous, nutty, almond flavouring and can be chopped
and roasted to be used in small quantities in fresh fruit salads or
scattered over the top of cream puddings.

> 1½ lb apricots
> ¾ lb granulated sugar

Halve the apricots, remove the stones and cut the flesh into very
thin slices. Arrange the apricot slices in a baking dish and pour over
the sugar. Cover with tinfoil and bake in a very moderate oven
(350° F. Reg. 4) for 20 minutes until all the sugar has melted.
Lower the oven to slow (300° F. Reg. 2) and continue cooking for
a further 1½ hours until the apricots are transparent and a lot of the
juice has been absorbed. Drain off and reserve the syrup and dry the
'chips' on greaseproof paper. Store them in an airtight polythene
container. The syrup can be used as a sauce for ice-cream or sponge
puddings.

Grapes with an Orange Custard Sauce

Orange custard, made with butter and really more like a fruit
cheese or curd than a true custard, was a popular sweet during the
seventeenth and eighteenth centuries. I added grapes to an original
recipe and came up with an ever-popular pudding which I serve
in locally made pottery goblets. A twentieth-century electric
liquidizer takes all the hard work out of this kind of antique
recipe.

Serves 6

> ½ lb green grapes (preferably the small
> seedless kind)
> Rind of 2 oranges
> Juice of 1 orange
> 1 tablespoon concentrated frozen orange juice
> 2 oz caster sugar
> 4 egg yolks
> 3 egg whites
> 8 oz unsalted butter

Halve the grapes and remove the seeds if necessary (leave the seedless variety whole). Divide the grapes between six goblets or large wine glasses.

Very thinly peel the rind of 2 oranges without incorporating any of the white membrane. Throw the peel into a saucepan of boiling water and boil for 20 minutes until soft. Purée the peel in an electric liquidizer or through a food mill (if you have neither of these, pound the peel to a paste in a pestle with a mortar). Add the sugar and orange juices, beating until the sugar has dissolved. Add the egg yolks and whites and liquidize or beat with a rotary whisk or electric beater until the mixture is thick and smooth.

Melt the butter and leave until cool but not beginning to harden. Add the melted butter to the egg and orange mixture and liquidize for 3 minutes or beat with a rotary whisk for 10 minutes. Cool in a refrigerator, beating occasionally, until thick and beginning to set. Pour the custard over the grapes and chill well before serving.

Melon Pot-pourri

Small, sweet melons used to grow in abundance in the hothouses of the great properties of Britain. Now we have to rely on those that are imported from countries with a warmer climate, but in this instance the substitutes are worthy ones, providing you choose fruit that gives off a pungent smell and is beginning to soften around the stalk.

Serves 4

4 small Ogen or Charantais melons
¼ lb ripe strawberries or raspberries
2 ripe apricots
1 large peach
2 teaspoons lemon juice
4 almonds cut into slivers
2 oz caster sugar
1 wine glass kirsch

Cut a small slice from the top of each melon and remove the seeds with a silver spoon to prevent any metallic taste. Scoop out the flesh of the melons and cut it into small dice. Cut the strawberries into thick slices. Peel and chop the apricots and the peach. Combine the fruit in a bowl, sprinkle over the lemon juice, sugar and kirsch and mix lightly. Return the fruit to the melon shells and chill well before serving. Sprinkle with roasted almonds just before bringing to the table.

Pears

British eating pears, especially Conference, are some of the best in the world. They also respond well to cooking and can be made into many subtle-tasting and delicate dishes. Use them when they are at the height of their season in September or October and therefore reasonably priced. Due to modern marketing procedure pears are usually sold when unripe, which is unfair to both their flavour and texture. Place them in a sunny windowsill for 3–4 days after buying them and see what a difference it makes.

Pears are usually poached for cooked dishes and the secret of success is not to cook them too much. They should always be very gently poached in whatever syrup is to be used and cooked only until the pears are tender (they should look almost translucent). If there is to be any delay between the peeling and cooking of the pears, squeeze a little lemon juice over them.

Pears in Nightdresses

Serves 4

> 4 large pears
> 2 oz icing sugar
> ½ pint apple juice
> Juice of 1 lemon
> 4 egg whites
> 8 oz caster sugar
> 3 tablespoons redcurrant jelly

Peel the pears but leave the stalks on. Combine the apple juice with the lemon juice in a saucepan, bring to the boil and drop in the pears. Simmer gently for 30 minutes. Drain the pears, reserving the juice, and roll them in icing sugar. Place the pears in a baking dish.

Beat the egg whites until stiff. Add half the caster sugar and continue beating until the mixture forms stiff peaks. Lightly fold in remaining sugar and spread the meringue mixture over the pears to make a thick coating. Bake in a hot oven (400° F. Reg. 6) for 10 minutes until the meringue is crisp and light golden in colour.

Combine the redcurrant jelly with the cooking liquid and bring to the boil. Cook over a high heat until the mixture is reduced by about a third. Serve the pears with the hot sauce.

Red Fruit Salad

A concoction of fresh fruits laced with brandy that can be made with a mixture of fresh and tinned fruit.

Serves 6

1 pint water
4 oz granulated sugar
Juice of 1 orange
¼ lb redcurrants (good ones can be bought in tins)
1 lb mixed red fruits as available:
cherries, firm eating plums, raspberries and strawberries
2 tablespoons brandy

Combine the sugar and water, bring to the boil and cook over a high heat until the syrup has been reduced by about one-third. Leave to cool and stir in the orange juice.

Prepare the fruit by slicing the plums, removing the stones of cherries, thickly slicing strawberries etc. Place them in a glass serving dish and pour over the syrup. Cover and refrigerate for 2 hours.

Add the brandy just before serving and serve well chilled with some sweetened whipped cream.

Apple Snow

Serves 4

1½ lb cooking apples
1 tablespoon lemon juice
2 tablespoons caster sugar
2 tablespoons water
2 egg whites
½ gill double cream

Peel, core and slice apples. Combine apples, lemon juice, sugar and water in a saucepan and cook over a low heat, stirring every now and then, for about 20 minutes until apples are soft and pulpy.

Mash them until smooth with a potato masher and check for sweetness; more sugar may have to be added, depending on the tartness of the apples. Set aside and leave to cool.

Whip egg whites until stiff. Lightly fold egg whites into the apple pulp and pile the mixture in four glass goblets. Whip the cream until thick and decorate each serving with a blob of cream. Serve well chilled.

Rich Trifle

Serves 4

6 trifle sponge cakes
4 tablespoons raspberry jam
Wine glass of medium-dry sherry
¼ lb macaroons
4 egg yolks
1 pint milk
1½ oz sugar
1 drop vanilla essence
¼ pint double cream
2 oz split almonds

Bring milk nearly up to the boil and remove from the heat. Beat the egg yolks with the sugar until smooth. Pour the hot milk on to the eggs, beating all the time. Put the custard into a clean pan and cook over a very low heat, stirring all the time with a wooden spoon, until the mixture thickens enough to coat the back of the spoon. Flavour with vanilla essence.

Split each cake in half, lengthways, and spread them with raspberry jam. Arrange the cakes in the bottom of a glass dish and cover with crumbled macaroons. Pour over the sherry and leave to stand for 30 minutes. Pour over the custard and leave to set in a refrigerator. Whip the cream until thick and spread it evenly over the top of the custard. Decorate the top of the trifle with split almonds roasted until golden brown in a hot oven.

Brandy Snaps with Banana Cream

Serves 4

8 brandy snaps
3 bananas
½ gill double cream

Peel and mash the bananas. Add the cream and beat with a whisk until the mixture is thick and smooth. Fill the brandy snaps with the banana cream.

Eighteenth-century Fool

A combination of trifle and syllabub that is very delicious. It must be made the day before required.

Serves 4

> 30 ratafias (small macaroons)
> ½ gill brandy
> 1 gill orange juice
> Juice of 2 lemons
> 4 oz caster sugar
> ½ pint double cream
> 1 tablespoon orange flower water
> (available from good chemists)
> 1 orange

Crumble the ratafias and place them in a glass bowl. Pour over the brandy. Combine the orange and lemon juice in a basin. Add the sugar and gradually beat in the cream, whisking until the mixture is light and frothy. Add the orange water and pour the mixture over the ratafias. Leave in a refrigerator overnight.

Peel the orange, divide the segments and remove all pith, membrane and skin. Decorate the pudding with the orange segments and serve well chilled.

Orange and Sherry Cream

The ideal topping for this delicious pudding is wild strawberries picked in the woods. Commercially or garden-grown strawberries will make an adequate second best.

Serves 4

> 1 pint double cream
> ½ oz gelatine
> Finely grated rind and juice of 2 oranges
> 3 oz caster sugar
> 3 tablespoons Bristol Cream Sherry
> (or a medium-dry sherry)

¼ pint double cream
1 drop vanilla essence
1 tablespoon caster sugar
¼ lb wild or garden strawberries

Combine the finely grated orange rind, 1 pint of cream and sugar in a saucepan and heat through until it is really hot but not boiling, and the sugar has melted. Remove from the heat.

Combine the gelatine and orange juice in a small saucepan and stir over a low heat until the gelatine is melted. Leave to cool. Stir the gelatine mixture and the sherry into the heated cream and mix well. Pour the mixture into four glass dishes or a glass bowl and chill in a refrigerator until set.

Whip ¼ pint double cream, mix in the vanilla essence and fold in 1 tablespoon caster sugar. Spread the whipped cream over the set orange sherry cream and decorate with fresh strawberries. Serve well chilled.

Stone Cream

Serves 6

¼ pint milk
½ oz (1 packet) gelatine
1 pint double cream
4 egg yolks
3 tablespoons raspberry or strawberry jam
2 oz shredded almonds

Combine the milk and gelatine in a small saucepan and stir over a low heat until the gelatine has melted (on no account boil the milk or the mixture will curdle). Beat the egg yolks until smooth. Heat the cream to just below boiling point and gradually beat it into the egg yolks. Blend in the milk and gelatine mixture.

Spread the jam over the bottom of a fireproof serving dish and pour over the custard mixture. Bake in a moderate oven (325° F. Reg. 3) for 30–45 minutes until the mixture has set. Leave to cool.

Spread the almonds on a baking sheet and cook in a hot oven (425° F. Reg. 7) for 2–3 minutes until golden brown. Cool and scatter the almonds over the top of the cooled cream. Serve chilled.

Strawberry Burnt Cream

Serves 4

8 oz strawberries
1 oz caster sugar
1 tablespoon brandy
1 tablespoon orange juice
¼ pint double cream
4 oz demerara sugar

Hull the strawberries, cut them into thick slices and arrange them in a shallow, fireproof baking dish. Sprinkle over the caster sugar, brandy and orange juice. Whip the cream until stiff and spread it evenly over the strawberries. Refrigerate for 2 hours in the ice-making compartment of the refrigerator or in a deep freeze. Sprinkle the brown sugar over the cream. Level the top with a knife.

Place the dish as near as possible to the highest heat of a grill, watching it closely and removing the dish as soon as the sugar melts and caramelises. Chill in the refrigerator and serve cold.

Strawberry Dream

Serves 6

4 egg whites
1 oz icing sugar
2 oz plain chocolate
1 lb ripe strawberries
2 oz caster sugar
½ pint double cream

Reserve some strawberries for decoration and mash the rest with a fork. Beat the cream until stiff and fold in the mashed strawberries and caster sugar. Coarsely grate the chocolate; beat the egg whites until stiff and then beat in the icing sugar and chocolate. Divide the strawberry mixture between six glass goblets, top with the egg white mixture, garnish with strawberries and chill before serving.

Syllabubs

The syllabub is one of the most delicious and light of all English country house puddings. Its history dates back to the Elizabethan days when it was made with foaming milk still warm from the cow. A genuine syllabub was made with champagne and its name, reputedly, comes from a combination of Sille, part of the Champagne country and 'bub' which was Elizabethan slang for a sparkling drink.

Not many people nowadays have either the means or the desire to chase a cow around a meadow with a milking stool in one hand and a bucket in the other just before a dinner party, so the twentieth-century syllabub is most often made by whipping cream, beating in wine and then adding any other flavourings that are desired.

Syllabub with Raspberries

Serves 6

¾ *lb raspberries*
4 oz caster sugar
Grated rind half lemon
Juice 1 lemon
¾ *pint double cream*
½ *pint sweet Chablis*
1 oz slivered almonds

Sprinkle half the sugar over the raspberries and mash them to a pulp with a fork. Add the lemon juice and rind and mix well. Whisk the cream until stiff and gradually beat in the remaining sugar and the wine poured in a thin steady stream (this is the sort of job for which one needs three hands or help – don't use an electric beater as that causes the cream to be overbeaten and become separated). The cream should be light and stiff enough to hold its shape. Lightly fold the raspberry pulp into the cream, spoon into glasses and chill for at least 1 hour.

Roast the almonds until golden brown in a hot oven, cool and sprinkle them over the syllabub just before serving.

Tarty Anne

Serves 4–6

1 lb cooking apples
1 lb rhubarb
4 oz granulated sugar
4 tablespoons water
Pinch cinnamon
Grated peel of 1 lemon
¼ pint double cream
2 oz split, blanched almonds

Peel, core and slice apples. Trim rhubarb and cut into 1-inch pieces. Combine fruit in a heavy saucepan with the cinnamon, lemon peel, sugar and water. Bring to the boil, cover tightly and simmer slowly for 30 minutes until the fruit is soft. Mix well with a fork and leave to cool.

Spoon the fruit into goblets and gently pour over the cream so that it floats in a thin layer above the fruit. Chill well and sprinkle with the almonds, lightly toasted in a hot oven until golden, just before serving.

TARTS AND PIES

Basic Sweet Pastry for Tarts and Pies

This is a short, fine pastry and difficult to handle unless it is well chilled in a refrigerator before being rolled out. Roll out on a well floured board and chill the case before baking. With practice, you can make the pastry into a thin, delicate crust that really does melt in the mouth and is a far cry from those heavy, soggy doughs one all too often associates with fruit tarts or pies.

Enough to line a 9-inch pie plate or for the topping of a largish pie

6 oz plain flour
1 dessertspoon sugar
3 oz unsalted butter
1 small egg yolk
Juice ¼ lemon
Ice cold water to mix

Combine the flour and sugar. Add the butter cut into small pieces and, using two knives, cut it into the flour until the mixture resembles coarse breadcrumbs. Add the egg yolk and mix well. Gradually add enough ice-cold water to make a firm dough. Knead lightly, wrap in a clean tea towel and chill in a refrigerator for 30 minutes. Roll out on a well floured board, using a rolling-pin that is generously coated with flour.

Almond Pastry

Almonds used to be a great ingredient of English cooking. Unfortunately, like so many things, they are now on the expensive side but we must be thankful for small mercies and, in this case, the small mercy is that now one is able to buy ground almonds rather than having to pound them to a paste in a giant mortar. The following pastry is delectable and goes especially well with summer fruits. At first you may find the pastry tricky to manipulate but once you have the knack, the rolling process becomes easier and a small quantity goes a long way.

Enough for 24 tartlet cases

$\frac{1}{2}$ *lb ground almonds*
2 *egg whites*
Pinch of salt
6 *oz caster sugar*
Flour

Beat the egg whites with the salt until stiff. Add the sugar and almonds and mix lightly until a stiff dough is formed. Generously flour a board and rolling-pin and roll out the dough as thinly as you can (ideally about $\frac{1}{8}$ inch thick). Cut out with a 3-inch pastry cutter and line well greased tartlet tins.

Bake in a moderate oven (350° F. Reg. 4) for 15–20 minutes until crisp and a light golden colour. Turn the tins upside down and tap sharply on the bottom to remove the cases the instant they are out of the oven. Cool on wire racks and fill with one of the following mixtures.

Strawberry Jelly Tartlets

This is ideal to make when strawberries are cheap and a little overripe.

Makes about 20 tartlets

Almond pastry tartlets
1 lb strawberries
6 oz caster sugar
½ oz gelatine
Juice of 1 lemon
¼ pint double cream
Drop of vanilla essence
1 tablespoon icing sugar

Hull the strawberries and cut out any blemished parts. Purée the fruit in an electric liquidizer or through a food mill.

Dissolve the gelatine in the lemon juice over a low heat. Add the gelatine mixture to the strawberries with the caster sugar and mix well. Chill in a refrigerator until the jelly is just beginning to set. Fill the tartlets with the strawberry mixture and top with the cream, whipped until stiff and flavoured with a little vanilla essence and icing sugar.

Strawberry and Redcurrant Tartlets

Makes about 20 tartlets

Almond pastry tartlets
1 lb firm ripe strawberries
(raspberries if preferred)
¼ lb redcurrant jelly
Juice ½ lemon
2 tablespoons red wine

Combine the redcurrant jelly, lemon juice and wine in a saucepan and stir over a low heat until the jelly has melted. Leave to cool but not set.

Hull the strawberries and cut them into thin slices. Fill the cases with strawberry slices, pour a little melted jelly over each one and leave in a cool place to set. Thick or clotted cream can be served separately.

Grape and Lemon Tartlets

Makes about 20 tartlets

Almond pastry tartlets
1 lb black or green grapes
Juice of 1 lemon
4 tablespoons white wine
3 tablespoons caster sugar
¼ oz (½ envelope or ½ tablespoon) gelatine

Halve the grapes and remove the pips (if the skin is tough this should also be removed but that is a fiddling and time-consuming job). Combine the lemon juice and white wine in a measuring jug and add enough water to make half a pint. Add the sugar and gelatine and cook over a low heat, stirring continually, until the gelatine is dissolved. Leave to cool and until the jelly begins to set. Arrange the grapes in the pastry cases and spoon a little of the jelly over each one. Leave to set in a cool place.

Apple Puff Turnovers

Serves 4

½ lb puff pastry (I use frozen)
1½ lb cooking apples
4 oz soft brown sugar
1 oz sultanas
2 oz butter
1 tablespoon lemon juice
1 egg, beaten

Peel, core and slice the apples. Melt the butter, add the apples, sugar, sultanas and lemon juice, and cook over a low heat, stirring every now and then until the apples are pulped and the mixture is thick and a rich dark colour. Set to one side and leave to cool completely.

Roll out the pastry to ⅛ inch thickness and cut into four circles. Put equal amounts of filling in the centre of each circle, damp the pastry edges with water, fold over and pinch edges together very firmly. Brush with beaten egg, make a small slit in the top of each turnover and bake in a hot oven (425° F. Reg. 7) for 20–25 minutes until the pastry has risen and is golden brown. Serve hot or cold with cream or custard.

Apple and Almond Pie

Serves 6–8

½ lb short-crust pastry
1 lb cooking apples
2 tablespoons raspberry jam
Juice of 1 large lemon
1 tablespoon flour
2 oz butter
2 oz caster sugar
2 oz ground almonds
2 eggs
A little caster sugar

Roll out the pastry to about ⅛ inch thickness. Line a deep pie dish with two-thirds of the pastry and spread with the jam. Peel, core and slice the apples, arrange them over the jam and sprinkle over the lemon juice.

Beat the butter with 2 oz caster sugar until light and creamy. Add 1 egg and beat well until the mixture is smooth. Combine the ground almonds with the flour, fold the dry ingredients into the egg mixture and spoon it over the top of the apples.

Beat the remaining egg. Brush the edges of the pie dish with beaten egg and cover with the remaining pastry. Bake in a hot oven (400° F. Reg. 6) for 30 minutes, covering the top of the pastry with greaseproof paper when it is golden. Brush the pastry with the remaining egg, sprinkle over a little caster sugar and return to the oven for a further 5–10 minutes. Serve hot with cream.

Bakewell Tart

I have never been to Bakewell in Derbyshire, but I have good reason to be grateful for its existence, for a home-made Bakewell Tart is one of my favourite dishes. Usually the tart is served more as a cake than a sweet but I find it a perfect ending to a meal, served slightly warm with lashings of cream. Most shop-bought Bakewell tarts are inclined to be dry and heavy; this do-it-yourself variation is light, succulent and generous with the raspberry jam layer.

Serves 6–8

Pastry
8 oz plain flour
4 oz butter
1 small egg
2 teaspoons caster sugar
A little ice-cold water

Filling
5 egg yolks
1 egg white
4 oz ground almonds
6 oz caster sugar
4 oz melted butter
4 heaped tablespoons raspberry jam

To make the pastry sieve the flour into a bowl. Add the sugar and 4 oz butter cut into small pieces and, using two sharp knives cut the butter into the flour until the mixture resembles coarse breadcrumbs. Add the egg, mix well with your hands and then mix in enough ice-cold water to make a firm dough. Knead lightly, wrap in a floured cloth and chill in a refrigerator for 30 minutes.

Roll the pastry out thinly on a floured board and line a 9-inch flan dish or tin. Spread the jam evenly over the bottom of the pastry case. Beat the egg yolks with the egg white until smooth and mix in the almonds, sugar and melted butter. Pour the mixture into the pastry case and bake in a hot oven (400° F. Reg. 6) for 10 minutes, then reduce the heat to moderate (350° F. Reg. 4) and cook for a further 15–20 minutes until the filling is set and a light golden brown.

Cornish Apple Pie

Serves 6

¾ lb short-crust pastry
1½ lb cooking apples
1 tablespoon plain flour
¼ teaspoon ground cloves
½ teaspoon cinnamon
3 oz granulated sugar
1 tablespoon water

1 oz butter
4 tablespoons clotted or double cream
Caster sugar and a pinch ground cinnamon

Lightly butter a 2-pint dish. Peel, core and slice the apples into the pie dish. Add flour, 3 oz of sugar, the ground cloves and cinnamon and mix well. Add the water and dot with butter. Place a pastry funnel in the centre.

Roll out the pastry to ¼ inch thickness. Damp the edges of the pie dish, put the pastry over the top and press the edges down firmly. Trim off any extra pastry and flute edges with a fork. Use excess pastry to make leaves for decorations. Cut two slits on either side of the funnel. Bake the pie in a hot oven (425° F. Reg. 7) for 15 minutes, then reduce the heat to moderately hot (350° F. Reg. 4) and continue cooking for a further 35 minutes.

Carefully spoon the clotted cream or cream through the slits in the top of the pie and sprinkle the pastry with a mixture of caster sugar and a pinch of cinnamon. Serve hot.

Lemon Custard Pie

Although this tastes very much like a traditional lemon meringue pie, a lemon custard is used instead of a classic lemon curd, making a lighter and far more economical pudding.

Serves 4–6

Basic sweet pastry (see page 194)
Juice and rind of 1 lemon
2 eggs, separated
½ oz butter
1 tablespoon flour
¼ pint milk
¼ pint double cream
4 oz caster sugar

Roll the pastry out thinly and line a 9-inch flan case. Chill before filling. Finely grate the lemon rind. Beat the egg yolks with the lemon juice and add the rind. Melt the butter over a low heat. Add the flour and 2 oz of sugar. Mix well. Gradually add the milk and then the cream, stirring continuously over a medium low heat until thick and smooth. Do not allow to boil. Remove from the heat and beat, a little at a time, into the yolks and lemon juice. Leave to cool.

Pour the custard mixture into the prepared flan case, cover with foil and bake for 30 minutes in a moderate oven (350° F. Reg. 4) for 30 minutes or until the custard is set and the pastry cooked. Remove the foil.

Beat the egg whites with the remaining sugar until stiff and spoon the meringue on to the custard. Bake in a warm oven (300° F. Reg. 2) for a further 15–20 minutes until the topping is crisp and a pale golden brown. Serve hot or cold with cream.

Pear and Blackberry Tart

Blackberries and the first English pears of the season coincide and neither of these fruits is expensive; their combined flavour is an act of nature so what could be better for an early autumn pudding?

Serves 4

¼ *lb short-crust or flaky pastry*
4 *large ripe pears*
¾ *pint water*
8 *oz sugar*
1 *egg yolk*
¼ *lb blackberry or bramble jelly*
Juice of 1 lemon
2 *teaspoons arrowroot*
¼ *gill double cream*

Roll the pastry out thinly and line a 7-inch flan case. Line the case inside with greaseproof paper, fill with dried peas or beans, chill in a refrigerator for 30 minutes and then bake in a hot oven (400° F. Reg. 6) until the pastry case is golden. Remove the paper and dried peas and leave to cool.

Combine the sugar and water in a large saucepan, bring to the boil and simmer for 10 minutes.

Peel the pears, add them to the syrup and cook gently for 30 minutes or until the pears are tender. Remove the pears with a slotted spoon. Cut two in half while still hot, remove the cores and pulp the flesh, then beat in the egg yolk and spread the mixture over the base of the flan case. Halve remaining pears, remove the cores and cut into thin slices. Arrange the slices over the pulped pears. Melt the blackberry jelly over a low heat and pour it over the pears.

Boil up the syrup the pears were cooked in until it is reduced by about one-third. Add a little of the syrup to the arrowroot and mix to a smooth paste. Add the mixture to the syrup with the lemon juice and cook, stirring continually, until thick and smooth. Cool, pour over the fruit and chill in a refrigerator until firm. Whip the cream until thick and spread it on top of the flan. Serve well chilled.

Soft Fruit Tart

In the north and west of England, wortleberries (known by various country names such as 'herts', 'whorts', 'bilberries' and 'blueberries') grow wild in the hedgerows. Picking them is a job for children and, as it requires patience, is a chore that I have found requires a financial bribe if it is to produce a respectable quantity of fruit. Cooking brings out the flavour of these delicious fruits and they respond well to a recipe such as this one.

Serves 4–6

> Basic sweet pastry (see page 194)
> 1½ lb wortleberries (loganberries,
> currants or rhubarb may be substituted)
> 6 oz caster sugar
> 4 tablespoons flour
> ¼ pint double cream
> 2 drops vanilla essence

Roll the pastry out thinly and line a 9-inch flan case. Combine 5 oz sugar with the flour and mix well. Add the berries and toss lightly. Spread the berries in the flan case, cover lightly with greaseproof paper and bake in a moderate oven (350° F. Reg. 4) for about 40 minutes or until the pastry is crisp and a pale golden brown. leave to cool.

Whip the cream until stiff and mix in the remaining sugar and the vanilla essence. Spoon the cream over the berries and serve well chilled.

Spiced Plum Tart with Cream

Serves 6

> *Basic sweet pastry (see page 194)*
> *1½ lb cooking plums*
> *10 oz caster sugar*
> *1 oz butter*
> *1 teaspoon powdered ginger*
> *½ teaspoon powdered cinnamon*
> *Juice ½ lemon*
> *¼ pint cream*

Halve the plums and remove the stones. Roll out the pastry and line a 9-inch flan tin. Arrange the plums, cut side down, in the case.

Combine 8 oz sugar, ginger and cinnamon and sprinkle the mixture over the plums. Pour over lemon juice. Dot with very small pieces of butter and bake in a moderate oven (350° F. Reg. 4) for 40 minutes. Leave to cool. Whip the cream with the remaining sugar and spread over the cooled tart.

PUDDINGS

Crystal Pudding

As fresh as its name, this pudding owes its success to the contrast of flavours and textures.

Serves 6

> *1 lb green grapes (preferably seedless)*
> *Brown sugar*
> *2 5 fl. oz cartons sour cream*
> *2 oz finely chopped blanched almonds*

Leave seedless grapes whole, halve grapes with pips and remove seeds. Divide grapes between six wine glasses and sprinkle a generous layer of brown sugar over the surface. Spread the sour cream in a flat layer over the top of the sugar.

Place the almonds on a baking sheet and roast in a hot oven for 2–3 minutes until golden brown. Cool and then scatter over the puddings. Chill in a refrigerator for at least 1 hour before serving.

Cumberland Pudding with Jam and Brandy Sauce

Serves 4

> 1 oz butter
> 1 oz caster sugar
> 1½ oz self-raising flour
> Pinch salt
> 1 egg
> ½ pint milk
> 4 tablespoons apricot jam
> 1 tablespoon brandy

Beat the butter with the sugar until the mixture is smooth and creamy. Add the flour and salt, mix well and then beat in the egg and milk and whisk until the mixture is smooth and light. Pour into a well-buttered fireproof dish and cook in a hot oven (400° F. Reg. 6) for 30 minutes.

Melt the apricot jam in a saucepan, add the brandy, mix well and serve the sauce hot with the pudding.

Derbyshire Pudding

A glorified Queen of Puddings with the sweetness of sponge cake as a base rather than the more mundane white bread.

Serves 4

> 1 packet trifle sponge cakes
> Strawberry jam
> ¼ gill apple juice
> 2 eggs
> ½ pint milk
> 1 oz caster sugar
> Few drops vanilla essence
> Finely grated peel of ½ lemon
> 2 oz caster sugar

Lightly butter a fireproof baking dish and spread a layer of jam over the bottom and sides. Split the sponge cakes in half lengthways and spread each half with jam. Place the sponge cakes, jam side up, in layers in the dish. Pour over the apple juice and leave to soak for 30 minutes.

Separate the eggs and beat the egg yolks. Bring the milk nearly to the boil and pour the hot milk over the yolks beating all the time with a wire whisk. Stir in 1 oz caster sugar and pour the mixture into a clean saucepan. Cook over a very low heat, stirring continually until the custard thickens enough to coat the back of a wooden spoon. Add 2 drops of vanilla essence and the lemon peel. Pour over the sponge cakes and leave to cool for 1 hour.

Whip the egg whites until stiff, fold in 2 oz caster sugar and continue to whip until the mixture stands in stiff peaks. Spread over the custard and bake in a hot oven (425° F. Reg. 7) until the meringue is golden brown and crisp. Serve hot or cold with cream.

Lemon Pudding

This beautiful pudding separates in the cooking process to a custardy, almost lemon curd base and the lightest possible sponge topping.

Serves 6

2 oz butter
8 oz caster sugar
Juice and finely grated rind of 1½ lemons
2 eggs, separated
½ pint milk
3 tablespoons self-raising flour
¼ pint double cream
1 tablespoon caster sugar

Combine the butter and 8 oz caster sugar and beat until light and fluffy. Add the lemon juice, rind and egg yolks and mix well. Blend in the milk and flour and beat again until the mixture is thick and smooth. Whisk the egg whites until stiff and fold them into the pudding mixture. Pour into a well-greased baking or soufflé dish and bake in a moderate oven (350° F. Reg. 4) for 40 minutes until the pudding is firm and golden brown on top. If the top begins to get too brown, cover it with a piece of greaseproof paper. Leave to cool.

Beat the cream until stiff and mix in 1 tablespoon sugar. Spread the whipped cream over the cooled pudding and chill in the refrigerator before serving.

Marmalade Pudding

Much lighter than the normal steamed pudding made with flour, this pudding has a delicacy that appeals as much to the female sex as it does to pudding-loving males.

Serves 6

6 oz sliced white bread with the crusts removed
1 pint milk
3 eggs, separated
3 oz caster sugar
2 tablespoons chunky marmalade
2 oz raisins

Coarsely grate the bread. Bring the milk to the boil and leave to cool. Pour the cooled milk over the breadcrumbs. Beat the egg yolks with the sugar until the mixture is light and pale yellow. Mix in the marmalade and lightly blend in the bread and milk.

Whip the egg whites until stiff and fold them into the bread mixture. Well grease a pudding basin, sprinkle the raisins over the bottom and pour in the pudding mixture. Set the basin in a large saucepan with water coming up to the level of the pudding inside the basin. Bring the water to the boil and then simmer very gently – the water should only just be moving – for 1 hour. Turn out the pudding and serve it with Creamy Marmalade Sauce (see page 155).

Osborne Pudding

Serves 4

4 slices stale brown bread (not granary)
Softened butter
2 tablespoons raspberry jam
¾ pint milk
2 eggs, lightly beaten
1 oz soft brown sugar

Remove the crusts from the bread, lightly butter the slices and spread them with jam. Lay the bread slices, jam side up, in a lightly buttered fireproof baking dish and sprinkle with the sugar.

Add the milk to the eggs and beat with a rotary whisk or electric beater until the mixture is smooth. Pour the custard over the eggs and leave to stand for 20 minutes. Bake the pudding in a moderate oven (350° F. Reg. 4) for 35–40 minutes until the custard has set.

Queen of Puddings

Serves 4

2 oz stale sponge cake crumbs
2 eggs, separated
½ pint milk
3 oz caster sugar
1 drop vanilla essence
3 tablespoons raspberry jam
Butter

Butter a 1½-pint pie dish and spread the cake crumbs in the bottom. Beat the egg yolks with 1 oz caster sugar. Heat the milk until it reaches boiling point, add the vanilla essence and pour the milk on to the egg yolks, beating continuously until the mixture is smooth and the yolk is completely incorporated into the milk. Strain the custard over the cake crumbs and bake in a moderate oven (350° F. Reg. 4) for about 30 minutes or until set.

Heat the jam over a low heat until melted and pour it over the set custard. Whip the egg whites until stiff, add 2 oz caster sugar and continue to whip until the mixture will stand in firm peaks. Spread the meringue over the jam and return to a very moderate oven (325° F. Reg. 3) for about 30 minutes or until the meringue is light golden in colour and crisp. Serve hot with fresh cream.

Six Light Puddings

Half pancake, half soufflé, baked in the oven and served with a delicious jam sauce, these puddings are the epitome of 'the way to a man's heart' – my man's, anyway. Except for the egg white whisking, they can be made in advance but once put into the oven they need accurate timing.

Serves 6

2 oz butter plus extra butter for greasing
2 heaped tablespoons plain flour
½ pint milk

3 oz caster sugar
2 drops vanilla essence
2 eggs, separated
4 tablespoons apricot jam
Juice 1 lemon
2 tablespoons water

Grease well six flat heatproof saucers about 6 inches in diameter. Beat the egg yolks until smooth.

Melt 2 oz butter in a saucepan. Add the flour and mix well. Mix in the sugar and gradually blend in the milk, stirring continually over a medium heat until the mixture is thick and smooth. Bring to the boil and simmer for 3 minutes. Remove from the heat, beat in the vanilla essence and leave to cool for a further 3 minutes and beat in the egg yolk. Whip the egg whites until stiff. Fold the egg whites lightly into the base mixture and divide between the saucers, spreading the mixture evenly across the surface of the dishes. Bake in a moderate oven (350° F. Reg. 4) for 25 minutes.

Combine the apricot jam, water and lemon juice in a saucepan, mix well and heat until bubbling. Remove the puddings from the saucers with a spatula, and pour jam sauce into the centre of each one. Fold in two and serve at once.

INDEX